TEACHER'S PET PUBLICATIONS

PUZZLE PACK
for
Mrs. Frisby and the Rats of NIMH

based on the book by
Robert C. O' Brien

Written by
Mary B. Collins

INTRODUCTION

If you already own the LitPlan for this title, this Puzzle Pack will refresh your Unit Resource Materials and Vocabulary Resource Materials sections plus give you additional materials you can substitute into the tests.If you do not already have a complete LitPlan, these pages will give you some supplemental materials to use with your own plan. There are two main groups of materials: one set for unit words (such as characters' names, symbols, places, etc.) and one set for vocabulary words associated with the book.

WORD LIST

There is a word list for both the unit words and the vocabulary words. These lists show you which words are being used in the materials and the clues or definitions being used for those words. You may want to give students a word list with clues/definitions to help them, or you may want students to only have a word list (without clues/definitions) if you want them to work a little harder. Both are available for duplication. The word lists can also be your "calling key" for the bingo games.

FILL IN THE BLANK AND MATCHING

There are 4 each of the fill in the blank and matching worksheets for both the unit and vocabulary words. These pages can be used either as extra worksheets for students or as objective parts of a unit test. They can be done individually if students need extra help or as a whole class activity to review the material covered.

MAGIC SQUARES

The magic squares not only reinforce the material covered but also work on reasoning and math skills. Many teachers have told us that their students really enjoy doing these!

WORD SEARCH PUZZLES

The word search words go in all directions, as indicated on your answer keys. Two of the word search puzzles have the clues listed rather than the words. This makes the puzzle a little more difficult, but it reinforces the material better. Two word search puzzles have words only for students who find the clue puzzles too difficult.

CROSSWORD PUZZLES

Both unit and vocabulary word sections have 4 crossword puzzles.

BINGO CARDS

There are 32 individual bingo cards for the unit words and 32 individual bingo cards for the vocabulary words. You can use your word list as a "call list," calling the words at random and marking them off of your list as you go, or you could use the flash cards by cutting them apart and drawing the words at random from a hat (or box or whatever). To make a better review, you might ask for the definition and spelling of each word as you call it out—or you could call out the definitions and have students tell you the words they need to look for on the puzzle.

JUGGLE LETTERS

The vocabulary juggle letter game is intended to help students learn the spellings of the words. One sheet has the definitions listed on it as an extra help for students who need it or to reinforce the definitions if you choose to do so.

FLASH CARDS

We've included a set of vocabulary flash cards you can duplicate, cut, and fold for your students. Some teachers make a few sets for general use by the class; others make a set for each student. Some teachers duplicate them for each student and have the students cut & fold their own. You can cut out just the words and put them in a hat, have each student pick out one word and write the definition and a sentence for that word. Students then swap words and papers, with the next student adding a sentence of his own under the last one. You can have students swap as many times as you like. Each time the student will read the sentences written prior to his own and then add a sentence. You can cut out the words and definitions separately and play "I Have; Who Has?" Each student in the room draws a word and definition. The first student says, "I have (the name of the word). Who has the definition?" The student with the definition reads it then says, "I have (the name of the vocabulary word she has). Who has the definition?" The round continues until all words and definitions have been given.

Mrs. Frisby and the Rats of NIMH Word List

No.	Word	Clue/Definition
1.	AGES	He makes powders and potions.
2.	AIR	Six of the mice were blown away by this in the duct.
3.	ARTHUR	Chief engineer of the rat colony
4.	BILLY	He captures Mrs. Frisby under a colander.
5.	BONIFACE	Estate where the rats stayed after NIMH
6.	BROOK	The Frisbys live near one in the summer.
7.	BRUTUS	Huge rat revived after breathing the gas.
8.	BUSH	Thorny covering over the entrance to the rat hole: rose ___
9.	CAGE	Justin read instructions telling how to open the ___ door.
10.	CAPACITY	The size of an animal's brain is no measure of its ___.
11.	CARELESS	The men said they could capture the rats because they had become ___.
12.	CHIPMUNKS	They tell Nicodemus to go to the owl.
13.	CHRISTMAS	The rats stole most of the lights after this holiday.
14.	CIVILIZATION	Nicodemus wants the rats to build their own ___, just like the Romans & others.
15.	COLANDER	Billy uses it as a rat trap.
16.	CONTROL	Group C was the ___ Group.
17.	DRAGON	Cat that killed Jonathan Frisby
18.	DUSK	Best time to talk to the owl
19.	EIGHT	Number of mice the rats freed from their cages
20.	ELECTROCUTED	Jenner and his group were ___ when trying to steal a motor.
21.	EYE	Nicodemus has a patch over his left one.
22.	FITZGIBBON	The farmer
23.	FRISBY	She puts the sleeping powder in the cat's bowl.
24.	GEORGE	Male assistant in the NIMH lab
25.	GORDON	Owner of the Boniface Estate
26.	HENDERSON	The local hardware store: ______'s
27.	HOUSE	The Frisbys must move from theirs in the garden.
28.	ISABELLA	Young female rat Mrs. Frisby encounters in the library
29.	JENNER	Nicodemus's best friend growing up
30.	JONATHAN	Mrs. Frisby's husband; also one of the mice
31.	JULIE	Dr. Schultz's female assistant
32.	JUSTIN	He helps Mrs. Frisby escape from Billy.
33.	LEE	The Frisbys' house needs to be moved to the ___ of the stone.
34.	LIBRARY	Where Mrs. Frisby waits for her first meeting with Nicodemus.
35.	MARTIN	Timothy's older brother
36.	MAZE	Set of corridors Nicodemus ran through while George watched
37.	MECHANIZED	___ RATS INVADE HARDWARE STORE
38.	MOUNTAINS	National forest where the rats decide to move while at Boniface: Thorn ___
39.	MOVING	Mrs. Frisby worries about this while Timothy is sick: ___ Day
40.	NEUROLOGIST	Dr. Schultz is one; expert on brains, nerves, intelligence
41.	NICODEMUS	Leader of the rats
42.	NIMH	Letters on the truck when Nicodemus & Jenner were captured
43.	OWL	Oldest animal in the woods; he gives advice
44.	PAUL	Farmer Fitzgibbon's oldest son
45.	PEOPLE	Nicodemus re-names the 'rat race' to the '___ race.'
46.	PIN	Part Farmer Fitzgibbon orders, which delays plowing: linch ___
47.	PLAN	Completion of it would eliminate stealing: The ___

No.	Word	Clue/Definition
48.	PLOW	Farming tool Nicodemus designs for the rats to use
49.	PNEUMONIA	Timothy's illness
50.	PORGY	Yellow canary, once the Fitzgibbons' pet
51.	POST	Location of Mrs. Frisby's hiding hole: fence ___
52.	RABIES	Paul thinks the Public Health Service is investigating this disease in rats.
53.	READING	Most important skill the rats learn in NIMH
54.	SCHULTZ	Doctor who runs NIMH
55.	SHOCK	Rats get this through the maze floor when they go the wrong way.
56.	SHREW	Mrs. Frisby's neighbor
57.	SPIDER	Creature that bit Timothy some time ago
58.	SPY	Isabella thinks Mrs. Frisby is one.
59.	STEALING	The Plan is to learn to live without ___.
60.	STUMP	Mrs. Frisby finds corn, nuts, and mushrooms there.
61.	SULLIVAN	Rat who recommends plugging into the house current for electricity
62.	THORN	Place Nicodemus wants to move the rat colony: ___ Valley
63.	THREAD	The rats used this when exploring the air ducts.
64.	THREE	Number of rat groups in the NIMH lab
65.	TOOLS	The real treasure the rats find in the Toy Tinker's truck
66.	TOY	Nicodemus & the rats found tools in his truck: ___ Tinker
67.	TRASH	The rats learned to remove it and clean the house to avoid being found.
68.	TWENTY	Number of rats that escaped from NIMH
69.	WRITE	The rats spent their time reading and learning to ___ at Boniface Estate.

____

1. Mrs. Frisby's neighbor

2. Number of rats that escaped from NIMH

3. Timothy's older brother

4. The Frisbys live near one in the summer.

5. Estate where the rats stayed after NIMH

6. The real treasure the rats find in the Toy Tinker's truck

7. Best time to talk to the owl

8. Leader of the rats

9. The Frisbys must move from theirs in the garden.

10. Isabella thinks Mrs. Frisby is one.

11. Owner of the Boniface Estate

12. Creature that bit Timothy some time ago

13. Yellow canary, once the Fitzgibbons' pet

14. Nicodemus has a patch over his left one.

15. The size of an animal's brain is no measure of its ___.

16. Young female rat Mrs. Frisby encounters in the library

17. Dr. Schultz is one; expert on brains, nerves, intelligence

18. The rats learned to remove it and clean the house to avoid
    being found.
19. Mrs. Frisby finds corn, nuts, and mushrooms there.

20. Doctor who runs NIMH

Mrs. Frisby and the Rats of NIMH Fill In The Blanks 1 Answer Key

SHREW
1. Mrs. Frisby's neighbor

TWENTY
2. Number of rats that escaped from NIMH

MARTIN
3. Timothy's older brother

BROOK
4. The Frisbys live near one in the summer.

BONIFACE
5. Estate where the rats stayed after NIMH

TOOLS
6. The real treasure the rats find in the Toy Tinker's truck

DUSK
7. Best time to talk to the owl

NICODEMUS
8. Leader of the rats

HOUSE
9. The Frisbys must move from theirs in the garden.

SPY
10. Isabella thinks Mrs. Frisby is one.

GORDON
11. Owner of the Boniface Estate

SPIDER
12. Creature that bit Timothy some time ago

PORGY
13. Yellow canary, once the Fitzgibbons' pet

EYE
14. Nicodemus has a patch over his left one.

CAPACITY
15. The size of an animal's brain is no measure of its ___.

ISABELLA
16. Young female rat Mrs. Frisby encounters in the library

NEUROLOGIST
17. Dr. Schultz is one; expert on brains, nerves, intelligence

TRASH
18. The rats learned to remove it and clean the house to avoid being found.

STUMP
19. Mrs. Frisby finds corn, nuts, and mushrooms there.

SCHULTZ
20. Doctor who runs NIMH

1. Nicodemus's best friend growing up

2. Paul thinks the Public Health Service is investigating this disease in rats.

3. Jenner and his group were ___ when trying to steal a motor.

4. Number of rat groups in the NIMH lab

5. Place Nicodemus wants to move the rat colony: ___ Valley

6. Most important skill the rats learn in NIMH

7. The rats used this when exploring the air ducts.

8. Letters on the truck when Nicodemus & Jenner were captured

9. Rats get this through the maze floor when they go the wrong way.

10. Number of rats that escaped from NIMH

11. Nicodemus re-names the 'rat race' to the '___ race.'

12. Group C was the ___ Group.

13. Leader of the rats

14. The rats stole most of the lights after this holiday.

15. Timothy's illness

16. Creature that bit Timothy some time ago

17. Mrs. Frisby worries about this while Timothy is sick: ___ Day

18. ___ RATS INVADE HARDWARE STORE

19. Cat that killed Jonathan Frisby

20. Nicodemus has a patch over his left one.

Mrs. Frisby and the Rats of NIMH Fill In The Blanks 2 Answer Key

JENNER	1. Nicodemus's best friend growing up
RABIES	2. Paul thinks the Public Health Service is investigating this disease in rats.
ELECTROCUTED	3. Jenner and his group were ___ when trying to steal a motor.
THREE	4. Number of rat groups in the NIMH lab
THORN	5. Place Nicodemus wants to move the rat colony: ___ Valley
READING	6. Most important skill the rats learn in NIMH
THREAD	7. The rats used this when exploring the air ducts.
NIMH	8. Letters on the truck when Nicodemus & Jenner were captured
SHOCK	9. Rats get this through the maze floor when they go the wrong way.
TWENTY	10. Number of rats that escaped from NIMH
PEOPLE	11. Nicodemus re-names the 'rat race' to the '___ race.'
CONTROL	12. Group C was the ___ Group.
NICODEMUS	13. Leader of the rats
CHRISTMAS	14. The rats stole most of the lights after this holiday.
PNEUMONIA	15. Timothy's illness
SPIDER	16. Creature that bit Timothy some time ago
MOVING	17. Mrs. Frisby worries about this while Timothy is sick: ___ Day
MECHANIZED	18. ___ RATS INVADE HARDWARE STORE
DRAGON	19. Cat that killed Jonathan Frisby
EYE	20. Nicodemus has a patch over his left one.

1. The rats learned to remove it and clean the house to avoid being found.
2. Nicodemus wants the rats to build their own ___, just like the Romans & others.
3. Mrs. Frisby's husband; also one of the mice
4. The local hardware store: ______'s
5. The rats stole most of the lights after this holiday.
6. Timothy's illness
7. Rat who recommends plugging into the house current for electricity
8. Number of rats that escaped from NIMH
9. Paul thinks the Public Health Service is investigating this disease in rats.
10. Set of corridors Nicodemus ran through while George watched
11. National forest where the rats decide to move while at Boniface: Thorn ___
12. Jenner and his group were ___ when trying to steal a motor.
13. Most important skill the rats learn in NIMH
14. Number of mice the rats freed from their cages
15. Oldest animal in the woods; he gives advice
16. Young female rat Mrs. Frisby encounters in the library
17. She puts the sleeping powder in the cat's bowl.
18. Creature that bit Timothy some time ago
19. The men said they could capture the rats because they had become ___.
20. Rats get this through the maze floor when they go the wrong way.

TRASH	1. The rats learned to remove it and clean the house to avoid being found.
CIVILIZATION	2. Nicodemus wants the rats to build their own ___, just like the Romans & others.
JONATHAN	3. Mrs. Frisby's husband; also one of the mice
HENDERSON	4. The local hardware store: ______'s
CHRISTMAS	5. The rats stole most of the lights after this holiday.
PNEUMONIA	6. Timothy's illness
SULLIVAN	7. Rat who recommends plugging into the house current for electricity
TWENTY	8. Number of rats that escaped from NIMH
RABIES	9. Paul thinks the Public Health Service is investigating this disease in rats.
MAZE	10. Set of corridors Nicodemus ran through while George watched
MOUNTAINS	11. National forest where the rats decide to move while at Boniface: Thorn ___
ELECTROCUTED	12. Jenner and his group were ___ when trying to steal a motor.
READING	13. Most important skill the rats learn in NIMH
EIGHT	14. Number of mice the rats freed from their cages
OWL	15. Oldest animal in the woods; he gives advice
ISABELLA	16. Young female rat Mrs. Frisby encounters in the library
FRISBY	17. She puts the sleeping powder in the cat's bowl.
SPIDER	18. Creature that bit Timothy some time ago
CARELESS	19. The men said they could capture the rats because they had become ___.
SHOCK	20. Rats get this through the maze floor when they go the wrong way.

Mrs. Frisby and the Rats of NIMH Fill In The Blanks 4

_______________ 1. Timothy's older brother

_______________ 2. Paul thinks the Public Health Service is investigating this
                     disease in rats.
_______________ 3. Cat that killed Jonathan Frisby

_______________ 4. Mrs. Frisby worries about this while Timothy is sick: ___ Day

_______________ 5. Rats get this through the maze floor when they go the wrong
                     way.
_______________ 6. Yellow canary, once the Fitzgibbons' pet

_______________ 7. Farming tool Nicodemus designs for the rats to use

_______________ 8. Chief engineer of the rat colony

_______________ 9. Billy uses it as a rat trap.

_______________ 10. Mrs. Frisby finds corn, nuts, and mushrooms there.

_______________ 11. He helps Mrs. Frisby escape from Billy.

_______________ 12. Isabella thinks Mrs. Frisby is one.

_______________ 13. The real treasure the rats find in the Toy Tinker's truck

_______________ 14. Rat who recommends plugging into the house current for
                     electricity
_______________ 15. Location of Mrs. Frisby's hiding hole: fence ___

_______________ 16. Nicodemus re-names the 'rat race' to the '___ race.'

_______________ 17. Best time to talk to the owl

_______________ 18. Mrs. Frisby's neighbor

_______________ 19. Oldest animal in the woods; he gives advice

_______________ 20. Farmer Fitzgibbon's oldest son

MARTIN	1. Timothy's older brother
RABIES	2. Paul thinks the Public Health Service is investigating this disease in rats.
DRAGON	3. Cat that killed Jonathan Frisby
MOVING	4. Mrs. Frisby worries about this while Timothy is sick: ___ Day
SHOCK	5. Rats get this through the maze floor when they go the wrong way.
PORGY	6. Yellow canary, once the Fitzgibbons' pet
PLOW	7. Farming tool Nicodemus designs for the rats to use
ARTHUR	8. Chief engineer of the rat colony
COLANDER	9. Billy uses it as a rat trap.
STUMP	10. Mrs. Frisby finds corn, nuts, and mushrooms there.
JUSTIN	11. He helps Mrs. Frisby escape from Billy.
SPY	12. Isabella thinks Mrs. Frisby is one.
TOOLS	13. The real treasure the rats find in the Toy Tinker's truck
SULLIVAN	14. Rat who recommends plugging into the house current for electricity
POST	15. Location of Mrs. Frisby's hiding hole: fence ___
PEOPLE	16. Nicodemus re-names the 'rat race' to the '___ race.'
DUSK	17. Best time to talk to the owl
SHREW	18. Mrs. Frisby's neighbor
OWL	19. Oldest animal in the woods; he gives advice
PAUL	20. Farmer Fitzgibbon's oldest son

Mrs. Frisby and the Rats of NIMH Matching 1

____ 1. PORGY	A. Isabella thinks Mrs. Frisby is one.
____ 2. CHRISTMAS	B. The Frisbys must move from theirs in the garden.
____ 3. SPY	C. Nicodemus re-names the 'rat race' to the '____ race.'
____ 4. NICODEMUS	D. Huge rat revived after breathing the gas.
____ 5. ISABELLA	E. Leader of the rats
____ 6. COLANDER	F. The rats stole most of the lights after this holiday.
____ 7. MARTIN	G. Yellow canary, once the Fitzgibbons' pet
____ 8. LIBRARY	H. Owner of the Boniface Estate
____ 9. HOUSE	I. The Frisbys' house needs to be moved to the ____ of the stone.
____10. SPIDER	J. The real treasure the rats find in the Toy Tinker's truck
____11. TOOLS	K. Young female rat Mrs. Frisby encounters in the library
____12. JUSTIN	L. Chief engineer of the rat colony
____13. SCHULTZ	M. Creature that bit Timothy some time ago
____14. EYE	N. Timothy's older brother
____15. RABIES	O. Number of rats that escaped from NIMH
____16. BRUTUS	P. Oldest animal in the woods; he gives advice
____17. LEE	Q. Paul thinks the Public Health Service is investigating this disease in rats.
____18. ARTHUR	R. Billy uses it as a rat trap.
____19. SHOCK	S. Where Mrs. Frisby waits for her first meeting with Nicodemus.
____20. TWENTY	T. Nicodemus has a patch over his left one.
____21. BROOK	U. She puts the sleeping powder in the cat's bowl.
____22. PEOPLE	V. Doctor who runs NIMH
____23. OWL	W. He helps Mrs. Frisby escape from Billy.
____24. FRISBY	X. The Frisbys live near one in the summer.
____25. GORDON	Y. Rats get this through the maze floor when they go the wrong way.

Mrs. Frisby and the Rats of NIMH Matching 1 Answer Key

G - 1. PORGY

F - 2. CHRISTMAS

A - 3. SPY

E - 4. NICODEMUS

K - 5. ISABELLA

R - 6. COLANDER

N - 7. MARTIN

S - 8. LIBRARY

B - 9. HOUSE

M -10. SPIDER

J - 11. TOOLS

W -12. JUSTIN

V -13. SCHULTZ

T -14. EYE

Q -15. RABIES

D -16. BRUTUS

I - 17. LEE

L - 18. ARTHUR

Y -19. SHOCK

O -20. TWENTY

X -21. BROOK

C -22. PEOPLE

P -23. OWL

U -24. FRISBY

H -25. GORDON

A. Isabella thinks Mrs. Frisby is one.

B. The Frisbys must move from theirs in the garden.

C. Nicodemus re-names the 'rat race' to the '___ race.'

D. Huge rat revived after breathing the gas.

E. Leader of the rats

F. The rats stole most of the lights after this holiday.

G. Yellow canary, once the Fitzgibbons' pet

H. Owner of the Boniface Estate

I. The Frisbys' house needs to be moved to the ___ of the stone.

J. The real treasure the rats find in the Toy Tinker's truck

K. Young female rat Mrs. Frisby encounters in the library

L. Chief engineer of the rat colony

M. Creature that bit Timothy some time ago

N. Timothy's older brother

O. Number of rats that escaped from NIMH

P. Oldest animal in the woods; he gives advice

Q. Paul thinks the Public Health Service is investigating this disease in rats.

R. Billy uses it as a rat trap.

S. Where Mrs. Frisby waits for her first meeting with Nicodemus.

T. Nicodemus has a patch over his left one.

U. She puts the sleeping powder in the cat's bowl.

V. Doctor who runs NIMH

W. He helps Mrs. Frisby escape from Billy.

X. The Frisbys live near one in the summer.

Y. Rats get this through the maze floor when they go the wrong way.

Mrs. Frisby and the Rats of NIMH Matching 2

___ 1. TWENTY	A. Nicodemus has a patch over his left one.
___ 2. HOUSE	B. Chief engineer of the rat colony
___ 3. EIGHT	C. The rats learned to remove it and clean the house to avoid being found.
___ 4. MECHANIZED	D. Nicodemus re-names the 'rat race' to the '___ race.'
___ 5. CHIPMUNKS	E. Number of rat groups in the NIMH lab
___ 6. JONATHAN	F. ___ RATS INVADE HARDWARE STORE
___ 7. TOOLS	G. Mrs. Frisby finds corn, nuts, and mushrooms there.
___ 8. NIMH	H. Number of rats that escaped from NIMH
___ 9. TRASH	I. Yellow canary, once the Fitzgibbons' pet
___10. EYE	J. Dr. Schultz's female assistant
___11. JULIE	K. They tell Nicodemus to go to the owl.
___12. SPIDER	L. Doctor who runs NIMH
___13. PEOPLE	M. The Frisbys must move from theirs in the garden.
___14. NEUROLOGIST	N. Dr. Schultz is one; expert on brains, nerves, intelligence
___15. PORGY	O. Mrs. Frisby's husband; also one of the mice
___16. THREAD	P. Letters on the truck when Nicodemus & Jenner were captured
___17. THREE	Q. He makes powders and potions.
___18. STUMP	R. Farming tool Nicodemus designs for the rats to use
___19. TOY	S. Nicodemus & the rats found tools in his truck: ___ Tinker
___20. AGES	T. He helps Mrs. Frisby escape from Billy.
___21. ARTHUR	U. The rats used this when exploring the air ducts.
___22. READING	V. Most important skill the rats learn in NIMH
___23. PLOW	W. Creature that bit Timothy some time ago
___24. SCHULTZ	X. The real treasure the rats find in the Toy Tinker's truck
___25. JUSTIN	Y. Number of mice the rats freed from their cages

Mrs. Frisby and the Rats of NIMH Matching 2 Answer Key

H - 1. TWENTY	A. Nicodemus has a patch over his left one.
M - 2. HOUSE	B. Chief engineer of the rat colony
Y - 3. EIGHT	C. The rats learned to remove it and clean the house to avoid being found.
F - 4. MECHANIZED	D. Nicodemus re-names the 'rat race' to the '___ race.'
K - 5. CHIPMUNKS	E. Number of rat groups in the NIMH lab
O - 6. JONATHAN	F. ___ RATS INVADE HARDWARE STORE
X - 7. TOOLS	G. Mrs. Frisby finds corn, nuts, and mushrooms there.
P - 8. NIMH	H. Number of rats that escaped from NIMH
C - 9. TRASH	I. Yellow canary, once the Fitzgibbons' pet
A -10. EYE	J. Dr. Schultz's female assistant
J - 11. JULIE	K. They tell Nicodemus to go to the owl.
W -12. SPIDER	L. Doctor who runs NIMH
D -13. PEOPLE	M. The Frisbys must move from theirs in the garden.
N -14. NEUROLOGIST	N. Dr. Schultz is one; expert on brains, nerves, intelligence
I - 15. PORGY	O. Mrs. Frisby's husband; also one of the mice
U -16. THREAD	P. Letters on the truck when Nicodemus & Jenner were captured
E -17. THREE	Q. He makes powders and potions.
G -18. STUMP	R. Farming tool Nicodemus designs for the rats to use
S -19. TOY	S. Nicodemus & the rats found tools in his truck: ___ Tinker
Q -20. AGES	T. He helps Mrs. Frisby escape from Billy.
B -21. ARTHUR	U. The rats used this when exploring the air ducts.
V -22. READING	V. Most important skill the rats learn in NIMH
R -23. PLOW	W. Creature that bit Timothy some time ago
L - 24. SCHULTZ	X. The real treasure the rats find in the Toy Tinker's truck
T -25. JUSTIN	Y. Number of mice the rats freed from their cages

Mrs. Frisby and the Rats of NIMH Matching 3

___ 1. FITZGIBBON

___ 2. PLAN

___ 3. MOVING

___ 4. ELECTROCUTED

___ 5. ISABELLA

___ 6. NICODEMUS

___ 7. GEORGE

___ 8. PNEUMONIA

___ 9. CARELESS

___10. PLOW

___11. SPY

___12. READING

___13. MECHANIZED

___14. JONATHAN

___15. SPIDER

___16. LEE

___17. TWENTY

___18. PORGY

___19. CAPACITY

___20. PEOPLE

___21. PIN

___22. TRASH

___23. DRAGON

___24. NEUROLOGIST

___25. GORDON

A. The Frisbys' house needs to be moved to the ___ of the stone.

B. ___ RATS INVADE HARDWARE STORE

C. Number of rats that escaped from NIMH

D. The farmer

E. Leader of the rats

F. Part Farmer Fitzgibbon orders, which delays plowing: linch ___

G. Cat that killed Jonathan Frisby

H. The rats learned to remove it and clean the house to avoid being found.

I. Most important skill the rats learn in NIMH

J. Nicodemus re-names the 'rat race' to the '___ race.'

K. Isabella thinks Mrs. Frisby is one.

L. Owner of the Boniface Estate

M. Mrs. Frisby worries about this while Timothy is sick: ___ Day

N. Jenner and his group were ___ when trying to steal a motor.

O. Dr. Schultz is one; expert on brains, nerves, intelligence

P. Male assistant in the NIMH lab

Q. Creature that bit Timothy some time ago

R. Young female rat Mrs. Frisby encounters in the library

S. The men said they could capture the rats because they had become ___.

T. Timothy's illness

U. Completion of it would eliminate stealing: The ___

V. The size of an animal's brain is no measure of its ___.

W. Farming tool Nicodemus designs for the rats to use

X. Mrs. Frisby's husband; also one of the mice

Y. Yellow canary, once the Fitzgibbons' pet

Mrs. Frisby and the Rats of NIMH Matching 3 Answer Key

D - 1. FITZGIBBON
U - 2. PLAN
M - 3. MOVING
N - 4. ELECTROCUTED
R - 5. ISABELLA
E - 6. NICODEMUS
P - 7. GEORGE
T - 8. PNEUMONIA
S - 9. CARELESS
W -10. PLOW
K -11. SPY
I - 12. READING
B -13. MECHANIZED
X -14. JONATHAN
Q -15. SPIDER
A -16. LEE
C -17. TWENTY
Y -18. PORGY
V -19. CAPACITY
J -20. PEOPLE
F -21. PIN
H -22. TRASH
G -23. DRAGON
O -24. NEUROLOGIST
L -25. GORDON

A. The Frisbys' house needs to be moved to the ___ of the stone.
B. ___ RATS INVADE HARDWARE STORE
C. Number of rats that escaped from NIMH
D. The farmer
E. Leader of the rats
F. Part Farmer Fitzgibbon orders, which delays plowing: linch ___
G. Cat that killed Jonathan Frisby
H. The rats learned to remove it and clean the house to avoid being found.
I. Most important skill the rats learn in NIMH
J. Nicodemus re-names the 'rat race' to the '___ race.'
K. Isabella thinks Mrs. Frisby is one.
L. Owner of the Boniface Estate
M. Mrs. Frisby worries about this while Timothy is sick: ___ Day
N. Jenner and his group were ___ when trying to steal a motor.
O. Dr. Schultz is one; expert on brains, nerves, intelligence
P. Male assistant in the NIMH lab
Q. Creature that bit Timothy some time ago
R. Young female rat Mrs. Frisby encounters in the library
S. The men said they could capture the rats because they had become ___.
T. Timothy's illness
U. Completion of it would eliminate stealing: The ___
V. The size of an animal's brain is no measure of its ___.
W. Farming tool Nicodemus designs for the rats to use
X. Mrs. Frisby's husband; also one of the mice
Y. Yellow canary, once the Fitzgibbons' pet

___ 1. BONIFACE

___ 2. CIVILIZATION

___ 3. CONTROL

___ 4. PAUL

___ 5. POST

___ 6. MAZE

___ 7. BRUTUS

___ 8. CARELESS

___ 9. JENNER

___10. PLOW

___11. OWL

___12. HOUSE

___13. EYE

___14. JUSTIN

___15. SULLIVAN

___16. NICODEMUS

___17. PORGY

___18. AGES

___19. THORN

___20. ELECTROCUTED

___21. CAGE

___22. DUSK

___23. FITZGIBBON

___24. COLANDER

___25. SCHULTZ

A. Yellow canary, once the Fitzgibbons' pet

B. Justin read instructions telling how to open the ___ door.

C. The Frisbys must move from theirs in the garden.

D. Jenner and his group were ___ when trying to steal a motor.

E. Billy uses it as a rat trap.

F. Leader of the rats

G. Place Nicodemus wants to move the rat colony: ___ Valley

H. The farmer

I. Nicodemus's best friend growing up

J. Group C was the ___ Group.

K. Doctor who runs NIMH

L. He makes powders and potions.

M. Oldest animal in the woods; he gives advice

N. Best time to talk to the owl

O. He helps Mrs. Frisby escape from Billy.

P. The men said they could capture the rats because they had become ___.

Q. Farming tool Nicodemus designs for the rats to use

R. Location of Mrs. Frisby's hiding hole: fence ___

S. Huge rat revived after breathing the gas.

T. Estate where the rats stayed after NIMH

U. Nicodemus has a patch over his left one.

V. Nicodemus wants the rats to build their own ___, just like the Romans & others.

W. Farmer Fitzgibbon's oldest son

X. Set of corridors Nicodemus ran through while George watched

Y. Rat who recommends plugging into the house current for electricity

Mrs. Frisby and the Rats of NIMH Matching 4 Answer Key

T - 1. BONIFACE

A. Yellow canary, once the Fitzgibbons' pet

V - 2. CIVILIZATION

B. Justin read instructions telling how to open the ___ door.

J - 3. CONTROL

C. The Frisbys must move from theirs in the garden.

W - 4. PAUL

D. Jenner and his group were ___ when trying to steal a motor.

R - 5. POST

E. Billy uses it as a rat trap.

X - 6. MAZE

F. Leader of the rats

S - 7. BRUTUS

G. Place Nicodemus wants to move the rat colony: ___ Valley

P - 8. CARELESS

H. The farmer

I - 9. JENNER

I. Nicodemus's best friend growing up

Q -10. PLOW

J. Group C was the ___ Group.

M -11. OWL

K. Doctor who runs NIMH

C -12. HOUSE

L. He makes powders and potions.

U -13. EYE

M. Oldest animal in the woods; he gives advice

O -14. JUSTIN

N. Best time to talk to the owl

Y -15. SULLIVAN

O. He helps Mrs. Frisby escape from Billy.

F -16. NICODEMUS

P. The men said they could capture the rats because they had become ___.

A -17. PORGY

Q. Farming tool Nicodemus designs for the rats to use

L -18. AGES

R. Location of Mrs. Frisby's hiding hole: fence ___

G -19. THORN

S. Huge rat revived after breathing the gas.

D -20. ELECTROCUTED

T. Estate where the rats stayed after NIMH

B -21. CAGE

U. Nicodemus has a patch over his left one.

N -22. DUSK

V. Nicodemus wants the rats to build their own ___, just like the Romans & others.

H -23. FITZGIBBON

W. Farmer Fitzgibbon's oldest son

E -24. COLANDER

X. Set of corridors Nicodemus ran through while George watched

K -25. SCHULTZ

Y. Rat who recommends plugging into the house current for electricity

Mrs. Frisby and the Rats of NIMH Magic Squares 1

Match the definition with the vocabulary word. Put your answers in the magic squares below. When your answers are correct, all columns and rows will add to the same number.

A. LIBRARY
B. STEALING
C. STUMP
D. CONTROL
E. MOUNTAINS
F. LEE

G. BUSH
H. OWL
I. PIN
J. THORN
K. MOVING
L. DUSK

M. GORDON
N. FRISBY
O. BONIFACE
P. CHIPMUNKS

1. She puts the sleeping powder in the cat's bowl.
2. Thorny covering over the entrance to the rat hole: rose ___
3. Best time to talk to the owl
4. Where Mrs. Frisby waits for her first meeting with Nicodemus.
5. Mrs. Frisby worries about this while Timothy is sick: ___ Day
6. The Plan is to learn to live without

   ___.
7. Owner of the Boniface Estate
8. Oldest animal in the woods; he gives advice

9. National forest where the rats decide to move while at Boniface: Thorn ___
10. They tell Nicodemus to go to the owl.
11. Mrs. Frisby finds corn, nuts, and mushrooms there.
12. Place Nicodemus wants to move the rat colony: ___ Valley
13. Group C was the ___ Group.
14. Part Farmer Fitzgibbon orders, which delays plowing: linch ___
15. The Frisbys' house needs to be moved to the ___ of the stone.
16. Estate where the rats stayed after NIMH

A=	B=	C=	D=
E=	F=	G=	H=
I=	J=	K=	L=
M=	N=	O=	P=

Mrs. Frisby and the Rats of NIMH Magic Squares 1 Answer Key

Match the definition with the vocabulary word. Put your answers in the magic squares below. When your answers are correct, all columns and rows will add to the same number.

A. LIBRARY
B. STEALING
C. STUMP
D. CONTROL
E. MOUNTAINS
F. LEE

G. BUSH
H. OWL
I. PIN
J. THORN
K. MOVING
L. DUSK

M. GORDON
N. FRISBY
O. BONIFACE
P. CHIPMUNKS

1. She puts the sleeping powder in the cat's bowl.
2. Thorny covering over the entrance to the rat hole: rose ___
3. Best time to talk to the owl
4. Where Mrs. Frisby waits for her first meeting with Nicodemus.
5. Mrs. Frisby worries about this while Timothy is sick: ___ Day
6. The Plan is to learn to live without ___.
7. Owner of the Boniface Estate
8. Oldest animal in the woods; he gives advice
9. National forest where the rats decide to move while at Boniface: Thorn ___
10. They tell Nicodemus to go to the owl.
11. Mrs. Frisby finds corn, nuts, and mushrooms there.
12. Place Nicodemus wants to move the rat colony: ___ Valley
13. Group C was the ___ Group.
14. Part Farmer Fitzgibbon orders, which delays plowing: linch ___
15. The Frisbys' house needs to be moved to the ___ of the stone.
16. Estate where the rats stayed after NIMH

A=4	B=6	C=11	D=13
E=9	F=15	G=2	H=8
I=14	J=12	K=5	L=3
M=7	N=1	O=16	P=10

Mrs. Frisby and the Rats of NIMH Magic Squares 2

Match the definition with the vocabulary word. Put your answers in the magic squares below. When your answers are correct, all columns and rows will add to the same number.

A. GEORGE
B. BONIFACE
C. FRISBY
D. BROOK
E. MARTIN
F. EIGHT

G. BILLY
H. FITZGIBBON
I. PLOW
J. HOUSE
K. NEUROLOGIST
L. PAUL

M. PORGY
N. ARTHUR
O. AIR
P. RABIES

1. The farmer
2. Yellow canary, once the Fitzgibbons' pet
3. Estate where the rats stayed after NIMH
4. Dr. Schultz is one; expert on brains, nerves, intelligence
5. The Frisbys must move from theirs in the garden.
6. She puts the sleeping powder in the cat's bowl.
7. Paul thinks the Public Health Service is investigating this disease in rats.
8. Timothy's older brother
9. Six of the mice were blown away by this in the duct.
10. Number of mice the rats freed from their cages
11. Farming tool Nicodemus designs for the rats to use
12. The Frisbys live near one in the summer.
13. Male assistant in the NIMH lab
14. Farmer Fitzgibbon's oldest son
15. He captures Mrs. Frisby under a colander.
16. Chief engineer of the rat colony

A=	B=	C=	D=
E=	F=	G=	H=
I=	J=	K=	L=
M=	N=	O=	P=

Mrs. Frisby and the Rats of NIMH Magic Squares 2 Answer Key

Match the definition with the vocabulary word. Put your answers in the magic squares below. When your answers are correct, all columns and rows will add to the same number.

A. GEORGE
B. BONIFACE
C. FRISBY
D. BROOK
E. MARTIN
F. EIGHT

G. BILLY
H. FITZGIBBON
I. PLOW
J. HOUSE
K. NEUROLOGIST
L. PAUL

M. PORGY
N. ARTHUR
O. AIR
P. RABIES

1. The farmer
2. Yellow canary, once the Fitzgibbons' pet
3. Estate where the rats stayed after NIMH
4. Dr. Schultz is one; expert on brains, nerves, intelligence
5. The Frisbys must move from theirs in the garden.
6. She puts the sleeping powder in the cat's bowl.
7. Paul thinks the Public Health Service is investigating this disease in rats.
8. Timothy's older brother
9. Six of the mice were blown away by this in the duct.
10. Number of mice the rats freed from their cages
11. Farming tool Nicodemus designs for the rats to use
12. The Frisbys live near one in the summer.
13. Male assistant in the NIMH lab
14. Farmer Fitzgibbon's oldest son
15. He captures Mrs. Frisby under a colander.
16. Chief engineer of the rat colony

A=13	B=3	C=6	D=12
E=8	F=10	G=15	H=1
I=11	J=5	K=4	L=14
M=2	N=16	O=9	P=7

Mrs. Frisby and the Rats of NIMH Magic Squares 3

Match the definition with the vocabulary word. Put your answers in the magic squares below. When your answers are correct, all columns and rows will add to the same number.

A. SHREW
B. WRITE
C. AIR
D. MOUNTAINS
E. MAZE
F. FITZGIBBON
G. PLOW
H. JENNER
I. SHOCK
J. DRAGON
K. ISABELLA
L. EIGHT
M. SPY
N. LEE
O. SCHULTZ
P. FRISBY

1. The farmer
2. Rats get this through the maze floor when they go the wrong way.
3. Doctor who runs NIMH
4. National forest where the rats decide to move while at Boniface: Thorn ___
5. Isabella thinks Mrs. Frisby is one.
6. The rats spent their time reading and learning to ___ at Boniface Estate.
7. Nicodemus's best friend growing up
8. Young female rat Mrs. Frisby encounters in the library
9. Six of the mice were blown away by this in the duct.
10. She puts the sleeping powder in the cat's bowl.
11. Cat that killed Jonathan Frisby
12. Set of corridors Nicodemus ran through while George watched
13. Number of mice the rats freed from their cages
14. Farming tool Nicodemus designs for the rats to use
15. Mrs. Frisby's neighbor
16. The Frisbys' house needs to be moved to the ___ of the stone.

A=	B=	C=	D=
E=	F=	G=	H=
I=	J=	K=	L=
M=	N=	O=	P=

Mrs. Frisby and the Rats of NIMH Magic Squares 3 Answer Key

Match the definition with the vocabulary word. Put your answers in the magic squares below. When your answers are correct, all columns and rows will add to the same number.

A. SHREW
B. WRITE
C. AIR
D. MOUNTAINS
E. MAZE
F. FITZGIBBON

G. PLOW
H. JENNER
I. SHOCK
J. DRAGON
K. ISABELLA
L. EIGHT

M. SPY
N. LEE
O. SCHULTZ
P. FRISBY

1. The farmer
2. Rats get this through the maze floor when they go the wrong way.
3. Doctor who runs NIMH
4. National forest where the rats decide to move while at Boniface: Thorn ___
5. Isabella thinks Mrs. Frisby is one.
6. The rats spent their time reading and learning to ___ at Boniface Estate.
7. Nicodemus's best friend growing up
8. Young female rat Mrs. Frisby encounters in the library
9. Six of the mice were blown away by this in the duct.
10. She puts the sleeping powder in the cat's bowl.
11. Cat that killed Jonathan Frisby
12. Set of corridors Nicodemus ran through while George watched
13. Number of mice the rats freed from their cages
14. Farming tool Nicodemus designs for the rats to use
15. Mrs. Frisby's neighbor
16. The Frisbys' house needs to be moved to the ___ of the stone.

A=15	B=6	C=9	D=4
E=12	F=1	G=14	H=7
I=2	J=11	K=8	L=13
M=5	N=16	O=3	P=10

Mrs. Frisby and the Rats of NIMH Magic Squares 4

Match the definition with the vocabulary word. Put your answers in the magic squares below. When your answers are correct, all columns and rows will add to the same number.

A. ISABELLA
B. WRITE
C. ARTHUR
D. THORN
E. COLANDER
F. STUMP

G. CONTROL
H. GORDON
I. SPIDER
J. POST
K. TOOLS
L. BRUTUS

M. EIGHT
N. RABIES
O. MECHANIZED
P. SCHULTZ

1. Number of mice the rats freed from their cages
2. Mrs. Frisby finds corn, nuts, and mushrooms there.
3. Owner of the Boniface Estate
4. ___ RATS INVADE HARDWARE STORE
5. Huge rat revived after breathing the gas.
6. Chief engineer of the rat colony
7. Young female rat Mrs. Frisby encounters in the library
8. Location of Mrs. Frisby's hiding hole: fence ___

9. The real treasure the rats find in the Toy Tinker's truck
10. Place Nicodemus wants to move the rat colony: ___ Valley
11. The rats spent their time reading and learning to ___ at Boniface Estate.
12. Creature that bit Timothy some time ago
13. Paul thinks the Public Health Service is investigating this disease in rats.
14. Billy uses it as a rat trap.
15. Group C was the ___ Group.
16. Doctor who runs NIMH

A=	B=	C=	D=
E=	F=	G=	H=
I=	J=	K=	L=
M=	N=	O=	P=

Mrs. Frisby and the Rats of NIMH Magic Squares 4 Answer Key

Match the definition with the vocabulary word. Put your answers in the magic squares below. When your answers are correct, all columns and rows will add to the same number.

A. ISABELLA
B. WRITE
C. ARTHUR
D. THORN
E. COLANDER
F. STUMP

G. CONTROL
H. GORDON
I. SPIDER
J. POST
K. TOOLS
L. BRUTUS

M. EIGHT
N. RABIES
O. MECHANIZED
P. SCHULTZ

1. Number of mice the rats freed from their cages
2. Mrs. Frisby finds corn, nuts, and mushrooms there.
3. Owner of the Boniface Estate
4. ___ RATS INVADE HARDWARE STORE
5. Huge rat revived after breathing the gas.
6. Chief engineer of the rat colony
7. Young female rat Mrs. Frisby encounters in the library
8. Location of Mrs. Frisby's hiding hole: fence ___

9. The real treasure the rats find in the Toy Tinker's truck
10. Place Nicodemus wants to move the rat colony: ___ Valley
11. The rats spent their time reading and learning to ___ at Boniface Estate.
12. Creature that bit Timothy some time ago
13. Paul thinks the Public Health Service is investigating this disease in rats.
14. Billy uses it as a rat trap.
15. Group C was the ___ Group.
16. Doctor who runs NIMH

A=7	B=11	C=6	D=10
E=14	F=2	G=15	H=3
I=12	J=8	K=9	L=5
M=1	N=13	O=4	P=16

Mrs. Frisby and the Rats of NIMH Word Search 1

```
B  R  U  T  U  S  T  B  D  C  T  C  C  E  W  B
G  O  R  D  O  N  S  H  R  E  W  H  H  I  R  F
Q  D  V  W  I  A  O  A  A  I  E  R  I  G  I  N
Z  T  L  T  S  H  P  L  G  L  N  I  P  H  T  S
L  R  R  G  V  T  J  L  O  U  T  S  M  T  E  X
T  A  H  W  P  A  L  E  N  J  Y  T  U  E  Y  E
M  S  S  M  O  N  V  B  N  Q  B  M  N  W  P  H
K  H  U  F  R  O  B  A  X  N  R  A  K  M  S  Q
Q  T  B  T  G  J  B  S  L  J  E  S  S  C  Y  M
S  E  G  A  Y  S  P  I  D  E  R  R  G  M  L  R
T  H  R  E  E  Y  B  W  N  R  I  N  B  O  L  H
W  E  O  W  Z  R  R  T  E  A  I  H  R  V  I  C
C  E  O  C  A  Z  E  K  G  D  F  T  K  I  B  G
M  L  Y  R  K  Z  P  L  A  N  N  S  B  N  T  J
P  B  Y  P  A  U  L  E  C  O  U  V  I  G  O  G
Q  N  I  M  H  K  R  H  C  D  L  P  D  B  Y  R
```

Best time to talk to the owl (4)
Cat that killed Jonathan Frisby (6)
Completion of it would eliminate stealing: The ___ (4)
Creature that bit Timothy some time ago (6)
Dr. Schultz's female assistant (5)
Farmer Fitzgibbon's oldest son (4)
Farming tool Nicodemus designs for the rats to use (4)
Group C was the ___ Group. (7)
He captures Mrs. Frisby under a colander. (5)
He makes powders and potions. (4)
Huge rat revived after breathing the gas. (6)
Isabella thinks Mrs. Frisby is one. (3)
Justin read instructions telling how to open the ___ door. (4)
Letters on the truck when Nicodemus & Jenner were captured (4)
Location of Mrs. Frisby's hiding hole: fence ___ (4)
Most important skill the rats learn in NIMH (7)
Mrs. Frisby finds corn, nuts, and mushrooms there. (5)
Mrs. Frisby worries about this while Timothy is sick: ___ Day (6)
Mrs. Frisby's husband; also one of the mice (8)
Mrs. Frisby's neighbor (5)
Nicodemus & the rats found tools in his truck: ___ Tinker (3)
Nicodemus has a patch over his left one. (3)
Nicodemus's best friend growing up (6)

Number of mice the rats freed from their cages (5)
Number of rat groups in the NIMH lab (5)
Number of rats that escaped from NIMH (6)
Oldest animal in the woods; he gives advice (3)
Owner of the Boniface Estate (6)
Part Farmer Fitzgibbon orders, which delays plowing: linch ___ (3)
Rats get this through the maze floor when they go the wrong way. (5)
Set of corridors Nicodemus ran through while George watched (4)
Six of the mice were blown away by this in the duct. (3)
The Frisbys' house needs to be moved to the ___ of the stone. (3)
The rats learned to remove it and clean the house to avoid being found. (5)
The rats spent their time reading and learning to ___ at Boniface Estate. (5)
The rats stole most of the lights after this holiday. (9)
They tell Nicodemus to go to the owl. (9)
Thorny covering over the entrance to the rat hole: rose ___ (4)
Timothy's older brother (6)
Where Mrs. Frisby waits for her first meeting with Nicodemus. (7)
Yellow canary, once the Fitzgibbons' pet (5)
Young female rat Mrs. Frisby encounters in the library (8)

Mrs. Frisby and the Rats of NIMH Word Search 1 Answer Key

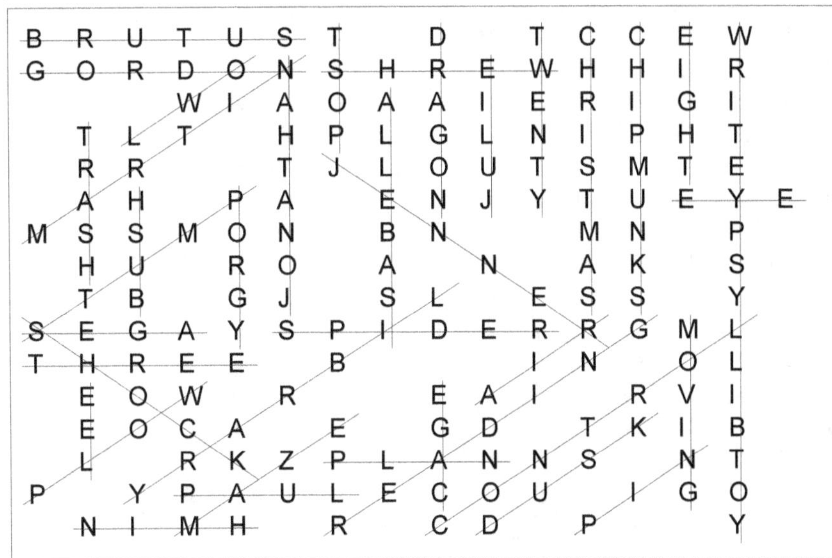

Best time to talk to the owl (4)

Cat that killed Jonathan Frisby (6)

Completion of it would eliminate stealing: The ___ (4)

Creature that bit Timothy some time ago (6)

Dr. Schultz's female assistant (5)

Farmer Fitzgibbon's oldest son (4)

Farming tool Nicodemus designs for the rats to use (4)

Group C was the ___ Group. (7)

He captures Mrs. Frisby under a colander. (5)

He makes powders and potions. (4)

Huge rat revived after breathing the gas. (6)

Isabella thinks Mrs. Frisby is one. (3)

Justin read instructions telling how to open the ___ door. (4)

Letters on the truck when Nicodemus & Jenner were captured (4)

Location of Mrs. Frisby's hiding hole: fence ___ (4)

Most important skill the rats learn in NIMH (7)

Mrs. Frisby finds corn, nuts, and mushrooms there. (5)

Mrs. Frisby worries about this while Timothy is sick: ___ Day (6)

Mrs. Frisby's husband; also one of the mice (8)

Mrs. Frisby's neighbor (5)

Nicodemus & the rats found tools in his truck: ___ Tinker (3)

Nicodemus has a patch over his left one. (3)

Nicodemus's best friend growing up (6)

Number of mice the rats freed from their cages (5)

Number of rat groups in the NIMH lab (5)

Number of rats that escaped from NIMH (6)

Oldest animal in the woods; he gives advice (3)

Owner of the Boniface Estate (6)

Part Farmer Fitzgibbon orders, which delays plowing: linch ___ (3)

Rats get this through the maze floor when they go the wrong way. (5)

Set of corridors Nicodemus ran through while George watched (4)

Six of the mice were blown away by this in the duct. (3)

The Frisbys' house needs to be moved to the ___ of the stone. (3)

The rats learned to remove it and clean the house to avoid being found. (5)

The rats spent their time reading and learning to ___ at Boniface Estate. (5)

The rats stole most of the lights after this holiday. (9)

They tell Nicodemus to go to the owl. (9)

Thorny covering over the entrance to the rat hole: rose ___ (4)

Timothy's older brother (6)

Where Mrs. Frisby waits for her first meeting with Nicodemus. (7)

Yellow canary, once the Fitzgibbons' pet (5)

Young female rat Mrs. Frisby encounters in the library (8)

Mrs. Frisby and the Rats of NIMH Word Search 2

```
B  I  L  L  Y  M  O  V  I  N  G  C  P  L  A  N
U  E  I  G  H  T  J  D  U  S  K  H  V  L  K  K
S  Y  J  C  P  N  E  U  M  O  N  I  A  T  O  L
H  G  F  G  E  K  S  S  S  W  M  P  S  T  H  W
T  R  O  T  O  L  H  E  F  T  T  M  N  M  F  J
D  O  C  W  P  M  R  I  Z  J  I  U  I  X  R  N
S  P  Y  A  L  L  E  B  A  S  I  N  N  P  I  N
S  W  G  U  E  Z  W  A  R  T  W  K  B  C  S  W
W  E  A  V  A  H  J  R  S  O  M  S  O  D  B  Q
S  P  R  M  N  O  Y  O  T  X  O  D  L  W  Y  X
U  M  E  T  N  U  J  Q  K  H  E  K  O  E  B  W
T  U  A  J  W  S  E  P  Y  M  O  K  R  E  E  H
U  T  D  U  W  E  N  P  U  M  A  R  T  I  N  P
R  S  I  L  X  T  N  S  O  P  Y  I  N  D  L  E
B  F  N  I  Q  X  E  T  K  S  R  V  O  K  Y  N
C  A  G  E  A  I  R  L  Y  W  T  F  C  E  Q  P
```

Best time to talk to the owl (4)

Completion of it would eliminate stealing: The ___ (4)

Dr. Schultz's female assistant (5)

Farmer Fitzgibbon's oldest son (4)

Farming tool Nicodemus designs for the rats to use (4)

Group C was the ___ Group. (7)

He captures Mrs. Frisby under a colander. (5)

He helps Mrs. Frisby escape from Billy. (6)

He makes powders and potions. (4)

Huge rat revived after breathing the gas. (6)

Isabella thinks Mrs. Frisby is one. (3)

Justin read instructions telling how to open the ___ door. (4)

Leader of the rats (9)

Letters on the truck when Nicodemus & Jenner were captured (4)

Location of Mrs. Frisby's hiding hole: fence ___ (4)

Most important skill the rats learn in NIMH (7)

Mrs. Frisby finds corn, nuts, and mushrooms there. (5)

Mrs. Frisby worries about this while Timothy is sick: ___ Day (6)

Mrs. Frisby's neighbor (5)

Nicodemus & the rats found tools in his truck: ___ Tinker (3)

Nicodemus has a patch over his left one. (3)

Nicodemus re-names the 'rat race' to the '___ race.' (6)

Nicodemus's best friend growing up (6)

Number of mice the rats freed from their cages (5)

Number of rats that escaped from NIMH (6)

Oldest animal in the woods; he gives advice (3)

Part Farmer Fitzgibbon orders, which delays plowing: linch ___ (3)

Paul thinks the Public Health Service is investigating this disease in rats. (6)

Place Nicodemus wants to move the rat colony: ___ Valley (5)

Set of corridors Nicodemus ran through while George watched (4)

She puts the sleeping powder in the cat's bowl. (6)

Six of the mice were blown away by this in the duct. (3)

The Frisbys live near one in the summer. (5)

The Frisbys must move from theirs in the garden. (5)

The Frisbys' house needs to be moved to the ___ of the stone. (3)

The rats spent their time reading and learning to ___ at Boniface Estate. (5)

They tell Nicodemus to go to the owl. (9)

Thorny covering over the entrance to the rat hole: rose ___ (4)

Timothy's illness (9)

Timothy's older brother (6)

Yellow canary, once the Fitzgibbons' pet (5)

Young female rat Mrs. Frisby encounters in the library (8)

Mrs. Frisby and the Rats of NIMH Word Search 2 Answer Key

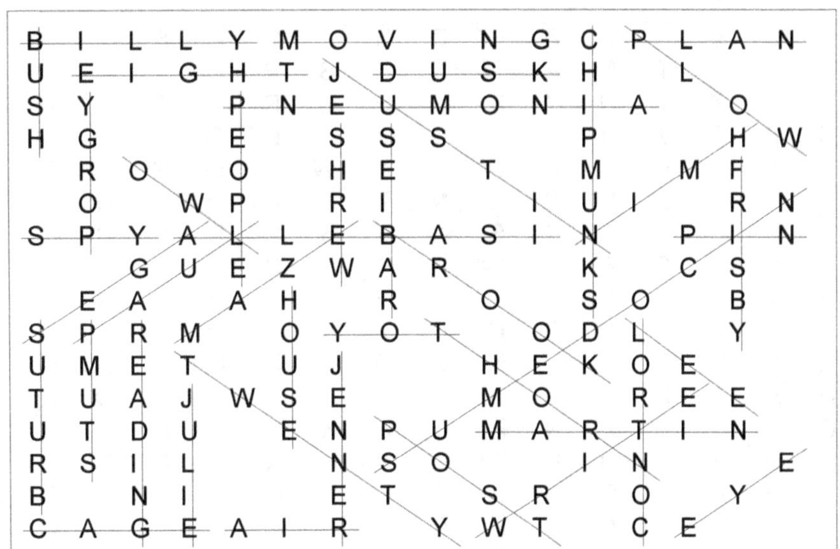

Best time to talk to the owl (4)

Completion of it would eliminate stealing: The ___ (4)

Dr. Schultz's female assistant (5)

Farmer Fitzgibbon's oldest son (4)

Farming tool Nicodemus designs for the rats to use (4)

Group C was the ___ Group. (7)

He captures Mrs. Frisby under a colander. (5)

He helps Mrs. Frisby escape from Billy. (6)

He makes powders and potions. (4)

Huge rat revived after breathing the gas. (6)

Isabella thinks Mrs. Frisby is one. (3)

Justin read instructions telling how to open the ___ door. (4)

Leader of the rats (9)

Letters on the truck when Nicodemus & Jenner were captured (4)

Location of Mrs. Frisby's hiding hole: fence ___ (4)

Most important skill the rats learn in NIMH (7)

Mrs. Frisby finds corn, nuts, and mushrooms there. (5)

Mrs. Frisby worries about this while Timothy is sick: ___ Day (6)

Mrs. Frisby's neighbor (5)

Nicodemus & the rats found tools in his truck: ___ Tinker (3)

Nicodemus has a patch over his left one. (3)

Nicodemus re-names the 'rat race' to the '___ race.' (6)

Nicodemus's best friend growing up (6)

Number of mice the rats freed from their cages (5)

Number of rats that escaped from NIMH (6)

Oldest animal in the woods; he gives advice (3)

Part Farmer Fitzgibbon orders, which delays plowing: linch ___ (3)

Paul thinks the Public Health Service is investigating this disease in rats. (6)

Place Nicodemus wants to move the rat colony: ___ Valley (5)

Set of corridors Nicodemus ran through while George watched (4)

She puts the sleeping powder in the cat's bowl. (6)

Six of the mice were blown away by this in the duct. (3)

The Frisbys live near one in the summer. (5)

The Frisbys must move from theirs in the garden. (5)

The Frisbys' house needs to be moved to the ___ of the stone. (3)

The rats spent their time reading and learning to ___ at Boniface Estate. (5)

They tell Nicodemus to go to the owl. (9)

Thorny covering over the entrance to the rat hole: rose ___ (4)

Timothy's illness (9)

Timothy's older brother (6)

Yellow canary, once the Fitzgibbons' pet (5)

Young female rat Mrs. Frisby encounters in the library (8)

```
S M E C H A N I Z E D S C S A S Y B J T
U C H R I S T M A S N I S P I T C O O P
L F H W H Z V N Y I V E H R N C O N N F
L I N U P S J V A I L V E E O O L I A L
I T D Y L T N T L E F N W F M N A F T S
V Z Q Y T T N I R C N T Z R U T N A H L
A G S X L U Z A X E C V S I E R D C A Z
N I Y H O A C B J W H W G S N O E E N Z
F B W M T S G C L P O M J B P L R K C J
R B T I E R A N R N U P A Y O T Y O H P
M O O R G P G T I N S W L R S O H O Y K
P N J H A J I S A B E L L A T H O R N D
H L I C C S Q X N R E U K H N I A B E Z
Z G I M N P H N H R L W R X J R N S Q E
E T E W H K I S D B X E R O B L B E Z P
Y G R O P T Q N E Z A M Z I L E I G H T
E P S L R N R O B D Y Z L B T O S A H K
M T T P R G Q G U S G D S I B E G N E G
O L E E S E E A S T U M P L C T R I K Z
V W A O P H A R H S Y A I L Z U L T S L
I B L P Y N O D K Q U C D Y H U Z S L T
N V I L L B G C I L F Q E T J W K U O R
G M N E D C G L K N O D R O G B J J O H
R V G B R U T U S N G A R A B I E S T B
```

AGES	COLANDER	JONATHAN	PAUL	SPIDER
AIR	CONTROL	JULIE	PEOPLE	SPY
ARTHUR	DRAGON	JUSTIN	PIN	STEALING
BILLY	DUSK	LEE	PLAN	STUMP
BONIFACE	EIGHT	LIBRARY	PLOW	SULLIVAN
BROOK	EYE	MARTIN	PNEUMONIA	THORN
BRUTUS	FITZGIBBON	MAZE	PORGY	THREAD
BUSH	FRISBY	MECHANIZED	POST	THREE
CAGE	GEORGE	MOUNTAINS	RABIES	TOOLS
CAPACITY	GORDON	MOVING	READING	TOY
CARELESS	HOUSE	NEUROLOGIST	SCHULTZ	TRASH
CHRISTMAS	ISABELLA	NIMH	SHOCK	TWENTY
CIVILIZATION	JENNER	OWL	SHREW	WRITE

AGES	COLANDER	JONATHAN	PAUL	SPIDER
AIR	CONTROL	JULIE	PEOPLE	SPY
ARTHUR	DRAGON	JUSTIN	PIN	STEALING
BILLY	DUSK	LEE	PLAN	STUMP
BONIFACE	EIGHT	LIBRARY	PLOW	SULLIVAN
BROOK	EYE	MARTIN	PNEUMONIA	THORN
BRUTUS	FITZGIBBON	MAZE	PORGY	THREAD
BUSH	FRISBY	MECHANIZED	POST	THREE
CAGE	GEORGE	MOUNTAINS	RABIES	TOOLS
CAPACITY	GORDON	MOVING	READING	TOY
CARELESS	HOUSE	NEUROLOGIST	SCHULTZ	TRASH
CHRISTMAS	ISABELLA	NIMH	SHOCK	TWENTY
CIVILIZATION	JENNER	OWL	SHREW	WRITE

Mrs. Frisby and the Rats of NIMH Word Search 4

```
S U L L I V A N P S R U H T R A D E F L
U X T K F B K V H S E L P L W Y C I R C
T S J M P I R S N H A X F N I E X G I F
U D Z M R L W O X O D C D A Q B N H S K
R S U L M L E F O C I X W L L Q R T B Z
B T B S P Y C G S K N U M P I H C A Y B
S E H T K D A Q C G G M L P O O X V R E
L A T R P N F G N I V O M B L S X B G Y
E L P W E I I Z C F W B V A C X T R M K
E I D N B E N I M H H X N S L O O T A G
T N G E E O O R R D Q D E S Q E S Y R B
R G K U D U B J A F E G Z E G H C K T T
A V H R W V M E E R A D X L R Z X I I V
S B O O Y G R O P N E M R E D I P S N P
H G W L U H K H N T N Y W R Z K N A N F
Q L C O T S C Y U I Q E E A T I J B O K
N J A G W C E C Y M A C R C A O T E S X
Z W G I K R O D R A G O N T J Y Y L R H
Y D E S R R I N Z M V S N H U U L L E Y
W H P T T N T T T B Q U L S S Z L A D Z
L S H C R G J G E R O Y U U T G V I N X
X P E O P L E Z A M O R A B I E S T E T
R L H J O N A T H A N L P Y N C K G H W
E T C A P A C I T Y N I C O D E M U S R
```

AGES	EIGHT	MAZE	READING
AIR	ELECTROCUTED	MOUNTAINS	SHOCK
ARTHUR	EYE	MOVING	SHREW
BILLY	FRISBY	NEUROLOGIST	SPIDER
BONIFACE	GEORGE	NICODEMUS	SPY
BROOK	GORDON	NIMH	STEALING
BRUTUS	HENDERSON	OWL	STUMP
BUSH	HOUSE	PAUL	SULLIVAN
CAGE	ISABELLA	PEOPLE	THORN
CAPACITY	JENNER	PIN	THREAD
CARELESS	JONATHAN	PLAN	THREE
CHIPMUNKS	JULIE	PLOW	TOOLS
COLANDER	JUSTIN	PNEUMONIA	TOY
CONTROL	LEE	PORGY	TRASH
DRAGON	LIBRARY	POST	TWENTY
DUSK	MARTIN	RABIES	WRITE

Mrs. Frisby and the Rats of NIMH Word Search 4 Answer Key

AGES	EIGHT	MAZE	READING
AIR	ELECTROCUTED	MOUNTAINS	SHOCK
ARTHUR	EYE	MOVING	SHREW
BILLY	FRISBY	NEUROLOGIST	SPIDER
BONIFACE	GEORGE	NICODEMUS	SPY
BROOK	GORDON	NIMH	STEALING
BRUTUS	HENDERSON	OWL	STUMP
BUSH	HOUSE	PAUL	SULLIVAN
CAGE	ISABELLA	PEOPLE	THORN
CAPACITY	JENNER	PIN	THREAD
CARELESS	JONATHAN	PLAN	THREE
CHIPMUNKS	JULIE	PLOW	TOOLS
COLANDER	JUSTIN	PNEUMONIA	TOY
CONTROL	LEE	PORGY	TRASH
DRAGON	LIBRARY	POST	TWENTY
DUSK	MARTIN	RABIES	WRITE

Mrs. Frisby and the Rats of NIMH Crossword 1

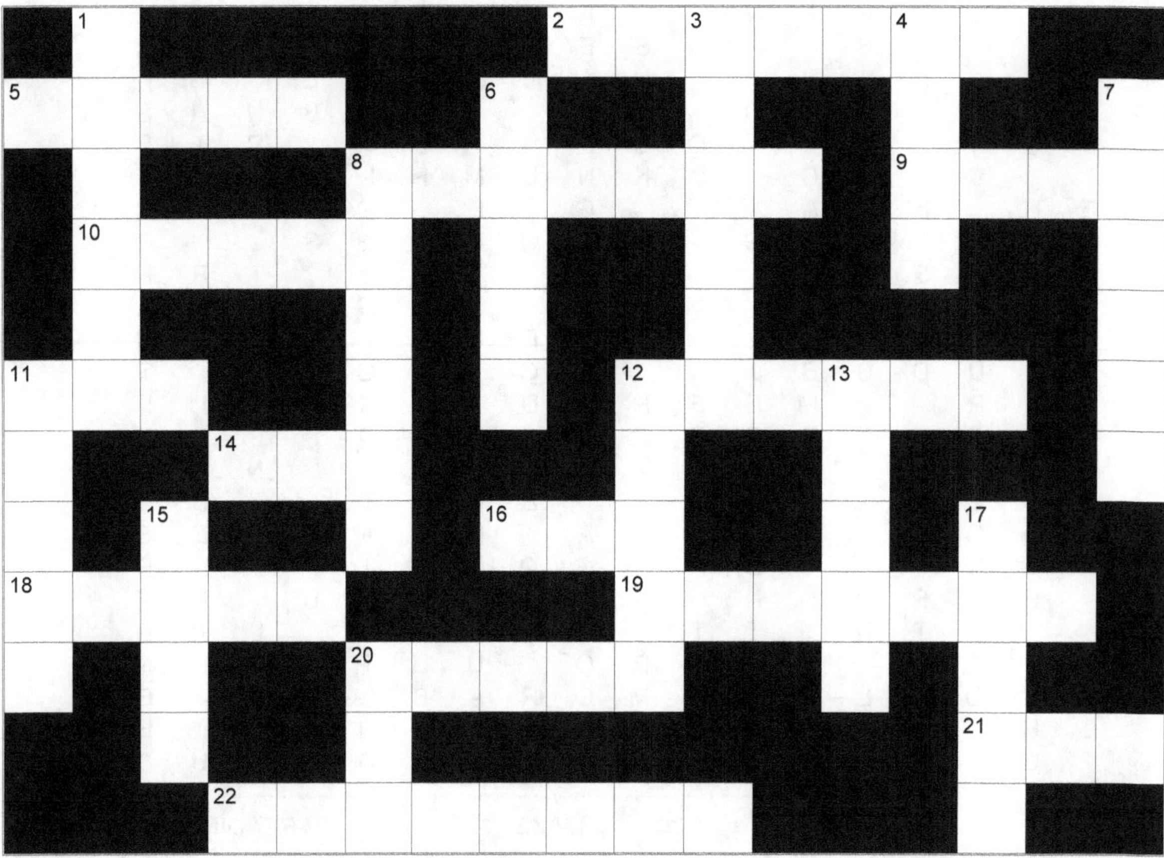

Across

2. Most important skill the rats learn in NIMH
5. The Frisbys live near one in the summer.
8. Doctor who runs NIMH
9. Set of corridors Nicodemus ran through while George watched
10. Mrs. Frisby finds corn, nuts, and mushrooms there.
11. Nicodemus has a patch over his left one.
12. Huge rat revived after breathing the gas.
14. The Frisbys' house needs to be moved to the ___ of the stone.
16. Oldest animal in the woods; he gives advice
18. The Frisbys must move from theirs in the garden.
19. Where Mrs. Frisby waits for her first meeting with Nicodemus.
20. Yellow canary, once the Fitzgibbons' pet
21. Nicodemus & the rats found tools in his truck: ___ Tinker
22. Estate where the rats stayed after NIMH

Down

1. She puts the sleeping powder in the cat's bowl.
3. Chief engineer of the rat colony
4. Letters on the truck when Nicodemus & Jenner were captured
6. Rats get this through the maze floor when they go the wrong way.
7. Male assistant in the NIMH lab
8. Creature that bit Timothy some time ago
11. Number of mice the rats freed from their cages
12. He captures Mrs. Frisby under a colander.
13. Place Nicodemus wants to move the rat colony: ___ Valley
15. Thorny covering over the entrance to the rat hole: rose ___
17. The rats spent their time reading and learning to ___ at Boniface Estate.
20. Part Farmer Fitzgibbon orders, which delays plowing: linch ___

The completed crossword grid contains the following answers:

- 2 Across: READING
- 5 Across: BROOK
- 8 Across: SCHULTZ
- 9 Across: MAZE
- 10 Across: STUMP
- 11 Across: EYE
- 12 Across: BRUTUS
- 14 Across: LEE
- 16 Across: OWL
- 18 Across: HOUSE
- 19 Across: LIBRARY
- 20 Across: PORGY
- 21 Across: TOY
- 22 Across: BONIFACE
- 3 Down: ARTHUR
- 4 Down: NIMH
- 7 Down: GEORGE

Across

2. Most important skill the rats learn in NIMH
5. The Frisbys live near one in the summer.
8. Doctor who runs NIMH
9. Set of corridors Nicodemus ran through while George watched
10. Mrs. Frisby finds corn, nuts, and mushrooms there.
11. Nicodemus has a patch over his left one.
12. Huge rat revived after breathing the gas.
14. The Frisbys' house needs to be moved to the ___ of the stone.
16. Oldest animal in the woods; he gives advice
18. The Frisbys must move from theirs in the garden.
19. Where Mrs. Frisby waits for her first meeting with Nicodemus.
20. Yellow canary, once the Fitzgibbons' pet
21. Nicodemus & the rats found tools in his truck: ___ Tinker
22. Estate where the rats stayed after NIMH

Down

1. She puts the sleeping powder in the cat's bowl.
3. Chief engineer of the rat colony
4. Letters on the truck when Nicodemus & Jenner were captured
6. Rats get this through the maze floor when they go the wrong way.
7. Male assistant in the NIMH lab
8. Creature that bit Timothy some time ago
11. Number of mice the rats freed from their cages
12. He captures Mrs. Frisby under a colander.
13. Place Nicodemus wants to move the rat colony: ___ Valley
15. Thorny covering over the entrance to the rat hole: rose ___
17. The rats spent their time reading and learning to ___ at Boniface Estate.
20. Part Farmer Fitzgibbon orders, which delays plowing: linch ___

Mrs. Frisby and the Rats of NIMH Crossword 2

Across

3. Set of corridors Nicodemus ran through while George watched
5. She puts the sleeping powder in the cat's bowl.
7. Number of mice the rats freed from their cages
10. The Frisbys must move from theirs in the garden.
12. Dr. Schultz's female assistant
13. Paul thinks the Public Health Service is investigating this disease in rats.
14. Completion of it would eliminate stealing: The ___
16. Part Farmer Fitzgibbon orders, which delays plowing: linch ___
17. Nicodemus & the rats found tools in his truck: ___ Tinker
18. The Frisbys live near one in the summer.
20. Isabella thinks Mrs. Frisby is one.
21. Rat who recommends plugging into the house current for electricity
22. Letters on the truck when Nicodemus & Jenner were captured

Down

1. The Frisbys' house needs to be moved to the ___ of the stone.
2. He makes powders and potions.
4. Nicodemus has a patch over his left one.
6. He captures Mrs. Frisby under a colander.
8. Place Nicodemus wants to move the rat colony: ___ Valley
9. Number of rats that escaped from NIMH
11. Creature that bit Timothy some time ago
12. Mrs. Frisby's husband; also one of the mice
14. Nicodemus re-names the 'rat race' to the '___ race.'
15. Six of the mice were blown away by this in the duct.
18. Thorny covering over the entrance to the rat hole: rose ___
19. Oldest animal in the woods; he gives advice

Mrs. Frisby and the Rats of NIMH Crossword 2 Answer Key

Across

3. Set of corridors Nicodemus ran through while George watched
5. She puts the sleeping powder in the cat's bowl.
7. Number of mice the rats freed from their cages
10. The Frisbys must move from theirs in the garden.
12. Dr. Schultz's female assistant
13. Paul thinks the Public Health Service is investigating this disease in rats.
14. Completion of it would eliminate stealing: The ___
16. Part Farmer Fitzgibbon orders, which delays plowing: linch ___
17. Nicodemus & the rats found tools in his truck: ___ Tinker
18. The Frisbys live near one in the summer.
20. Isabella thinks Mrs. Frisby is one.
21. Rat who recommends plugging into the house current for electricity
22. Letters on the truck when Nicodemus & Jenner were captured

Down

1. The Frisbys' house needs to be moved to the ___ of the stone.
2. He makes powders and potions.
4. Nicodemus has a patch over his left one.
6. He captures Mrs. Frisby under a colander.
8. Place Nicodemus wants to move the rat colony: ___ Valley
9. Number of rats that escaped from NIMH
11. Creature that bit Timothy some time ago
12. Mrs. Frisby's husband; also one of the mice
14. Nicodemus re-names the 'rat race' to the '___ race.'
15. Six of the mice were blown away by this in the duct.
18. Thorny covering over the entrance to the rat hole: rose ___
19. Oldest animal in the woods; he gives advice

Mrs. Frisby and the Rats of NIMH Crossword 3

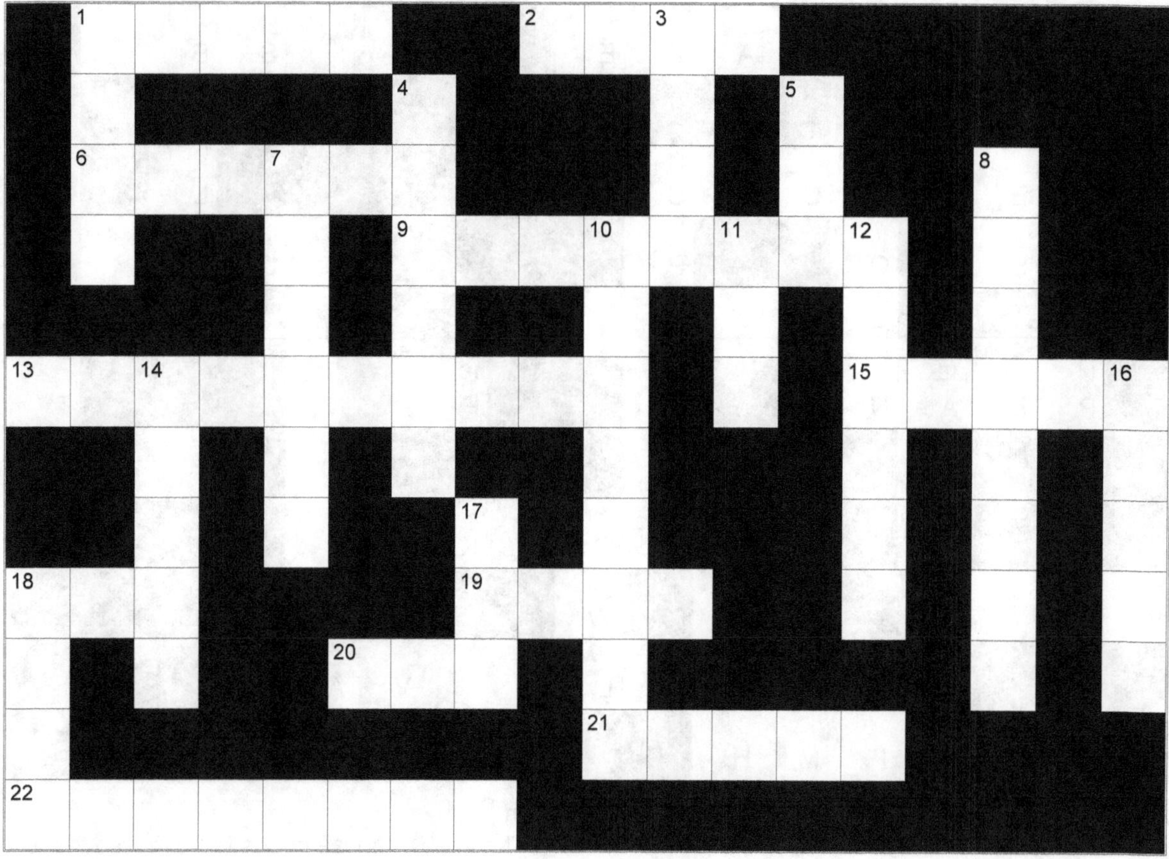

Across

1. The Frisbys live near one in the summer.
2. Letters on the truck when Nicodemus & Jenner were captured
6. Creature that bit Timothy some time ago
9. Young female rat Mrs. Frisby encounters in the library
13. The farmer
15. The rats learned to remove it and clean the house to avoid being found.
18. Six of the mice were blown away by this in the duct.
19. Completion of it would eliminate stealing: The ___
20. Nicodemus & the rats found tools in his truck: ___ Tinker
21. Number of mice the rats freed from their cages
22. Rat who recommends plugging into the house current for electricity

Down

1. Thorny covering over the entrance to the rat hole: rose ___
3. Set of corridors Nicodemus ran through while George watched
4. She puts the sleeping powder in the cat's bowl.
5. Oldest animal in the woods; he gives advice
7. Cat that killed Jonathan Frisby
8. Mrs. Frisby's husband; also one of the mice
10. Estate where the rats stayed after NIMH
11. The Frisbys' house needs to be moved to the ___ of the stone.
12. Chief engineer of the rat colony
14. Place Nicodemus wants to move the rat colony: ___ Valley
16. The Frisbys must move from theirs in the garden.
17. Isabella thinks Mrs. Frisby is one.
18. He makes powders and potions.

Mrs. Frisby and the Rats of NIMH Crossword 3 Answer Key

Across
1. The Frisbys live near one in the summer.
2. Letters on the truck when Nicodemus & Jenner were captured
6. Creature that bit Timothy some time ago
9. Young female rat Mrs. Frisby encounters in the library
13. The farmer
15. The rats learned to remove it and clean the house to avoid being found.
18. Six of the mice were blown away by this in the duct.
19. Completion of it would eliminate stealing: The ___
20. Nicodemus & the rats found tools in his truck: ___ Tinker
21. Number of mice the rats freed from their cages
22. Rat who recommends plugging into the house current for electricity

Down
1. Thorny covering over the entrance to the rat hole: rose ___
3. Set of corridors Nicodemus ran through while George watched
4. She puts the sleeping powder in the cat's bowl.
5. Oldest animal in the woods; he gives advice
7. Cat that killed Jonathan Frisby
8. Mrs. Frisby's husband; also one of the mice
10. Estate where the rats stayed after NIMH
11. The Frisbys' house needs to be moved to the ___ of the stone.
12. Chief engineer of the rat colony
14. Place Nicodemus wants to move the rat colony: ___ Valley
16. The Frisbys must move from theirs in the garden.
17. Isabella thinks Mrs. Frisby is one.
18. He makes powders and potions.

Across

1. Leader of the rats
4. Number of mice the rats freed from their cages
6. Rats get this through the maze floor when they go the wrong way.
8. Isabella thinks Mrs. Frisby is one.
10. Part Farmer Fitzgibbon orders, which delays plowing: linch ___
11. Oldest animal in the woods; he gives advice
12. The rats used this when exploring the air ducts.
13. Dr. Schultz's female assistant
15. Six of the mice were blown away by this in the duct.
16. Place Nicodemus wants to move the rat colony: ___ Valley
17. Letters on the truck when Nicodemus & Jenner were captured
19. Creature that bit Timothy some time ago
21. Most important skill the rats learn in NIMH

Down

1. Dr. Schultz is one; expert on brains, nerves, intelligence
2. Nicodemus wants the rats to build their own ___, just like the Romans & others.
3. Best time to talk to the owl
5. Number of rats that escaped from NIMH
7. The rats stole most of the lights after this holiday.
9. Farmer Fitzgibbon's oldest son
10. Timothy's illness
12. Nicodemus & the rats found tools in his truck: ___ Tinker
13. Nicodemus's best friend growing up
14. Mrs. Frisby worries about this while Timothy is sick: ___ Day
18. Justin read instructions telling how to open the ___ door.
20. Nicodemus has a patch over his left one.

Mrs. Frisby and the Rats of NIMH Crossword 4 Answer Key

1		2		3							4				5
N	I	C	O	D	E	M	U	S			E	I	G	H	T
E		I		U											W
U	V			6 S	H	O	7 C	K		8 S	9 P	Y			E
R		I		K			H				A		10 P	I	N
11 O	W	L			12 T	H	R	E	A	D	U			N	T
L		I				O	I		13 J	U	L	I	E		Y
O		Z			Y		S	14 M	E				U		
G		15 A	I	R		16 T	H	O	R	N	17 N	I	M	H	
I		T				M		V		N			O		18 C
19 S	P	20 I	D	E	R	A		I		E			N		A
T		O		Y		S		N		21 R	E	A	D	I	N G
		N		E		G		G					A		E

Across

1. Leader of the rats
4. Number of mice the rats freed from their cages
6. Rats get this through the maze floor when they go the wrong way.
8. Isabella thinks Mrs. Frisby is one.
10. Part Farmer Fitzgibbon orders, which delays plowing: linch ___
11. Oldest animal in the woods; he gives advice
12. The rats used this when exploring the air ducts.
13. Dr. Schultz's female assistant
15. Six of the mice were blown away by this in the duct.
16. Place Nicodemus wants to move the rat colony: ___ Valley
17. Letters on the truck when Nicodemus & Jenner were captured
19. Creature that bit Timothy some time ago
21. Most important skill the rats learn in NIMH

Down

1. Dr. Schultz is one; expert on brains, nerves, intelligence
2. Nicodemus wants the rats to build their own ___, just like the Romans & others.
3. Best time to talk to the owl
5. Number of rats that escaped from NIMH
7. The rats stole most of the lights after this holiday.
9. Farmer Fitzgibbon's oldest son
10. Timothy's illness
12. Nicodemus & the rats found tools in his truck: ___ Tinker
13. Nicodemus's best friend growing up
14. Mrs. Frisby worries about this while Timothy is sick: ___ Day
18. Justin read instructions telling how to open the ___ door.
20. Nicodemus has a patch over his left one.

Mrs Frisby

BUSH	PEOPLE	ARTHUR	FITZGIBBON	SULLIVAN
STEALING	GEORGE	CAPACITY	BILLY	LEE
EIGHT	NEUROLOGIST	FREE SPACE	DUSK	TWENTY
SHOCK	BRUTUS	AIR	TOY	MECHANIZED
CHIPMUNKS	SCHULTZ	THREAD	CARELESS	JENNER

Mrs Frisby

CAGE	CONTROL	THREE	MOVING	CIVILIZATION
PLAN	SHREW	HENDERSON	NIMH	MOUNTAINS
BROOK	THORN	FREE SPACE	MAZE	MARTIN
NICODEMUS	POST	READING	PLOW	AGES
COLANDER	JULIE	PIN	RABIES	BONIFACE

Mrs Frisby

ISABELLA	TRASH	SPIDER	DRAGON	MECHANIZED
BRUTUS	CARELESS	JULIE	AGES	LIBRARY
THREE	JONATHAN	FREE SPACE	PLAN	FRISBY
CAGE	LEE	SULLIVAN	PORGY	PLOW
AIR	THREAD	WRITE	BROOK	CONTROL

Mrs Frisby

SHOCK	MARTIN	GORDON	TWENTY	GEORGE
EYE	STUMP	HENDERSON	EIGHT	NIMH
SPY	COLANDER	FREE SPACE	STEALING	PIN
HOUSE	BUSH	CIVILIZATION	CHRISTMAS	THORN
NEUROLOGIST	READING	SCHULTZ	FITZGIBBON	CAPACITY

Mrs Frisby

SPY	TOY	ELECTROCUTED	JENNER	NEUROLOGIST
JULIE	ISABELLA	DUSK	STEALING	BRUTUS
TOOLS	SHREW	FREE SPACE	JUSTIN	TWENTY
THREE	NIMH	SPIDER	BILLY	HENDERSON
CARELESS	LEE	COLANDER	RABIES	BUSH

Mrs Frisby

FITZGIBBON	HOUSE	READING	MAZE	SHOCK
PNEUMONIA	EYE	SULLIVAN	AIR	MARTIN
PAUL	MOVING	FREE SPACE	CONTROL	CAPACITY
FRISBY	BROOK	PLOW	SCHULTZ	THREAD
WRITE	MOUNTAINS	DRAGON	MECHANIZED	GEORGE

Mrs Frisby

THREE	READING	BROOK	PEOPLE	TOOLS
PORGY	JENNER	SPIDER	SPY	BUSH
STUMP	SCHULTZ	FREE SPACE	ISABELLA	THORN
SHREW	CONTROL	ELECTROCUTED	MOUNTAINS	TOY
NICODEMUS	CAPACITY	MOVING	EIGHT	HENDERSON

Mrs Frisby

WRITE	FRISBY	PNEUMONIA	JUSTIN	TWENTY
ARTHUR	DRAGON	DUSK	STEALING	MARTIN
POST	THREAD	FREE SPACE	GEORGE	SULLIVAN
FITZGIBBON	PAUL	LEE	OWL	PLOW
COLANDER	JULIE	CIVILIZATION	PLAN	BONIFACE

Mrs Frisby

HENDERSON	JONATHAN	PEOPLE	RABIES	PORGY
SULLIVAN	MOUNTAINS	CAGE	SHREW	EYE
STEALING	TRASH	FREE SPACE	PNEUMONIA	WRITE
FRISBY	JUSTIN	NEUROLOGIST	AIR	GORDON
CARELESS	MAZE	PLAN	DUSK	SPIDER

Mrs Frisby

MECHANIZED	NICODEMUS	SHOCK	THREE	NIMH
HOUSE	OWL	BROOK	JULIE	ISABELLA
EIGHT	READING	FREE SPACE	SPY	CHRISTMAS
THREAD	THORN	TOY	STUMP	CIVILIZATION
COLANDER	BUSH	ELECTROCUTED	LEE	ARTHUR

Mrs Frisby

PIN	SULLIVAN	BUSH	CAPACITY	RABIES
CONTROL	BRUTUS	AIR	TRASH	OWL
GORDON	SCHULTZ	FREE SPACE	MAZE	THREAD
STEALING	NIMH	LEE	DRAGON	STUMP
PLOW	JENNER	PORGY	FRISBY	CHRISTMAS

Mrs Frisby

CARELESS	TWENTY	ELECTROCUTED	THREE	JULIE
HENDERSON	TOY	MARTIN	MOVING	NEUROLOGIST
BONIFACE	FITZGIBBON	FREE SPACE	READING	HOUSE
NICODEMUS	WRITE	CHIPMUNKS	ISABELLA	EIGHT
JUSTIN	PNEUMONIA	JONATHAN	CAGE	LIBRARY

Mrs Frisby

STUMP	SULLIVAN	TOY	BILLY	BUSH
RABIES	HOUSE	THREAD	MARTIN	NEUROLOGIST
SCHULTZ	CONTROL	FREE SPACE	CAPACITY	PLOW
LIBRARY	JENNER	PAUL	MECHANIZED	PLAN
NICODEMUS	EYE	PNEUMONIA	SHOCK	JULIE

Mrs Frisby

READING	AIR	TRASH	CARELESS	THREE
GORDON	BONIFACE	SHREW	MOUNTAINS	SPIDER
NIMH	PIN	FREE SPACE	COLANDER	WRITE
BRUTUS	CAGE	PEOPLE	MAZE	CIVILIZATION
DRAGON	POST	THORN	AGES	GEORGE

Mrs Frisby

THREAD	FITZGIBBON	AIR	ARTHUR	GORDON
TOOLS	MECHANIZED	LEE	FRISBY	MARTIN
EIGHT	CAGE	FREE SPACE	CARELESS	THREE
BROOK	ELECTROCUTED	BILLY	CIVILIZATION	GEORGE
LIBRARY	STEALING	WRITE	NICODEMUS	CAPACITY

Mrs Frisby

PORGY	RABIES	OWL	TRASH	BUSH
COLANDER	SHOCK	BRUTUS	POST	SPY
SCHULTZ	PAUL	FREE SPACE	TWENTY	CONTROL
MOVING	SULLIVAN	JENNER	BONIFACE	JONATHAN
CHIPMUNKS	TOY	DUSK	MOUNTAINS	SHREW

FITZGIBBON	SCHULTZ	CHIPMUNKS	MECHANIZED	SHREW
SULLIVAN	PEOPLE	MAZE	SPIDER	FRISBY
GEORGE	AIR	FREE SPACE	THORN	LEE
READING	COLANDER	JONATHAN	DUSK	PNEUMONIA
MOUNTAINS	TOY	POST	OWL	SPY

Mrs Frisby

BROOK	STEALING	MOVING	EYE	DRAGON
HOUSE	CARELESS	BONIFACE	PORGY	EIGHT
PIN	AGES	FREE SPACE	ELECTROCUTED	ISABELLA
CHRISTMAS	PAUL	ARTHUR	PLAN	LIBRARY
SHOCK	JULIE	THREE	CIVILIZATION	NEUROLOGIST

Mrs Frisby

LEE	BILLY	BRUTUS	BUSH	HOUSE
TRASH	GEORGE	JUSTIN	CHIPMUNKS	NIMH
PLAN	CAPACITY	FREE SPACE	THREE	JENNER
SULLIVAN	SHOCK	STEALING	DUSK	HENDERSON
THORN	NEUROLOGIST	READING	RABIES	FRISBY

Mrs Frisby

SPY	MOUNTAINS	JULIE	AGES	PNEUMONIA
STUMP	PORGY	PIN	ISABELLA	GORDON
TOOLS	PAUL	FREE SPACE	NICODEMUS	TWENTY
BONIFACE	TOY	FITZGIBBON	WRITE	COLANDER
OWL	CARELESS	MAZE	ELECTROCUTED	MECHANIZED

Mrs Frisby

STEALING	BILLY	FITZGIBBON	AIR	WRITE
PNEUMONIA	BRUTUS	OWL	LIBRARY	BONIFACE
DRAGON	SPIDER	FREE SPACE	JONATHAN	SHOCK
EYE	NIMH	BROOK	SPY	MOUNTAINS
JULIE	PLAN	CONTROL	NEUROLOGIST	TOOLS

Mrs Frisby

MARTIN	CHRISTMAS	ARTHUR	EIGHT	ELECTROCUTED
TWENTY	SULLIVAN	GORDON	MOVING	TRASH
GEORGE	CAGE	FREE SPACE	THREE	JUSTIN
SCHULTZ	AGES	PORGY	PIN	CIVILIZATION
THORN	MECHANIZED	MAZE	STUMP	TOY

NEUROLOGIST	SCHULTZ	STUMP	THREE	JUSTIN
CAGE	JONATHAN	TRASH	SHOCK	PEOPLE
GEORGE	SHREW	FREE SPACE	BUSH	OWL
BONIFACE	FITZGIBBON	CAPACITY	PORGY	CHRISTMAS
ARTHUR	PNEUMONIA	MOUNTAINS	JENNER	COLANDER

Mrs Frisby

DUSK	TWENTY	TOY	READING	SULLIVAN
SPY	FRISBY	AGES	ISABELLA	JULIE
HENDERSON	EYE	FREE SPACE	AIR	THORN
BILLY	EIGHT	MOVING	WRITE	TOOLS
LEE	MARTIN	CHIPMUNKS	LIBRARY	RABIES

TOOLS	STUMP	EIGHT	COLANDER	JUSTIN
BILLY	AIR	DRAGON	PLAN	EYE
BONIFACE	TRASH	FREE SPACE	HENDERSON	PIN
CHRISTMAS	THORN	SPIDER	BUSH	AGES
LEE	NEUROLOGIST	THREE	NICODEMUS	JENNER

Mrs Frisby

PAUL	LIBRARY	SHREW	PLOW	SCHULTZ
MOVING	PEOPLE	JULIE	SPY	WRITE
SULLIVAN	DUSK	FREE SPACE	JONATHAN	BROOK
CAGE	OWL	FITZGIBBON	CIVILIZATION	NIMH
CHIPMUNKS	CAPACITY	ISABELLA	THREAD	PNEUMONIA

Mrs Frisby

CHRISTMAS	DRAGON	ELECTROCUTED	GORDON	BONIFACE
AIR	DUSK	PAUL	STUMP	ISABELLA
NICODEMUS	PLAN	FREE SPACE	ARTHUR	LIBRARY
PNEUMONIA	OWL	LEE	FRISBY	CONTROL
CAGE	SPIDER	HENDERSON	CAPACITY	POST

Mrs Frisby

TOOLS	COLANDER	THORN	WRITE	SULLIVAN
SPY	AGES	TWENTY	GEORGE	BUSH
MOVING	BROOK	FREE SPACE	SHOCK	PIN
JUSTIN	THREAD	JONATHAN	STEALING	JULIE
TRASH	RABIES	SHREW	BRUTUS	MOUNTAINS

Mrs Frisby

LEE	READING	SPIDER	LIBRARY	STUMP
HENDERSON	CONTROL	CARELESS	PLOW	PLAN
CAGE	MOUNTAINS	FREE SPACE	FITZGIBBON	AGES
TWENTY	RABIES	CAPACITY	SPY	MARTIN
THREAD	BROOK	HOUSE	PEOPLE	DRAGON

Mrs Frisby

STEALING	NIMH	BILLY	COLANDER	AIR
PORGY	GEORGE	JONATHAN	TOOLS	BRUTUS
THORN	TOY	FREE SPACE	CHIPMUNKS	TRASH
DUSK	JENNER	BUSH	PNEUMONIA	CHRISTMAS
MAZE	CIVILIZATION	POST	FRISBY	ELECTROCUTED

Mrs Frisby

THREE	COLANDER	TWENTY	RABIES	TOY
THREAD	PAUL	SHOCK	STEALING	HOUSE
EYE	PIN	FREE SPACE	JENNER	GEORGE
HENDERSON	MARTIN	BROOK	WRITE	CONTROL
PORGY	ELECTROCUTED	PLAN	JUSTIN	DRAGON

Mrs Frisby

OWL	PEOPLE	NEUROLOGIST	STUMP	MOUNTAINS
CARELESS	SHREW	SPY	CAPACITY	BONIFACE
SPIDER	POST	FREE SPACE	NICODEMUS	MECHANIZED
CAGE	CIVILIZATION	MOVING	TRASH	NIMH
FRISBY	LIBRARY	BILLY	DUSK	CHRISTMAS

Mrs. Frisby Vocabulary Word List

No.	Word	Clue/Definition
1.	ABREAST	Side by side; beside each other in a line
2.	ABRUPTLY	Suddenly or unexpectedly
3.	ADJOURNED	Suspended (a meeting) until a later time or another place
4.	ADMONISHED	Mildly scolded; spoken to in disapproval
5.	AGITATED	Troubled or nervous
6.	ARTIFICIAL	Made by human work or art, not by nature
7.	ASTONISHED	Filled with sudden, overpowering surprise or wonder
8.	ASTUTE	Having or showing a clever or shrewd mind
9.	AUTHORITATIVELY	In a commanding way
10.	BEWILDERMENT	The condition of being completely puzzled
11.	CAPTIVITY	Imprisonment
12.	CIRCUMSTANCES	Conditions surrounding an event
13.	CLUTTERED	Containing too many things, often unorganized
14.	COLANDER	Strainer; a perforated pan used for draining liquids
15.	COMPILED	Made of materials from various sources
16.	COMRADESHIP	Friendship; companionship
17.	CONCEALED	Hidden
18.	CONFER	Discuss
19.	CONSTERNATION	Feeling of helplessness due to great fear or shock
20.	CONTOUR	The outline of a figure, mass, land, etc.
21.	CONVERGED	Came together to meet at a point or in a line
22.	CORDIAL	Courteous; gracious; friendly
23.	CORRIDOR	Passageway giving access to rooms, apartments, etc.
24.	CRYPTICALLY	In a manner that is mysterious or obscure in meaning
25.	CULTIVATED	Prepared for growing crops; tended; nurtured
26.	CURSORY	Performed rapidly with little attention to detail
27.	CYNICAL	Believing that people are only motivated by selfishness
28.	DEBRIS	Bits and pieces of rubbish; litter
29.	DEFECTIVE	Imperfect; faulty
30.	DELIBERATELY	Intentionally; on purpose; with forethought
31.	DESCENT	The moving from a higher to a lower place
32.	DESPAIRINGLY	In a manner feeling or showing hopelessness
33.	DICTATED	Spoken or read aloud to be written or recorded
34.	DISCONTENT	Dissatisfaction; a restless desire for something more
35.	DISPATCHED	Sent off on a specific errand
36.	DREADFULLY	Terribly
37.	DRONING	Making a continuous, low, monotonous sound
38.	DUSK	Period of partial darkness between day and night as the sun begins to set
39.	EAVES	Overhanging edges of a roof
40.	EAVESDROP	Listen secretly to a private conversation
41.	ELEGANTLY	In a splendid or luxurious style or design
42.	EMERGED	Came forth
43.	EPIDEMIC	Prevalent and spreading rapidly among many individuals
44.	EXERT	Put forth or use energetically
45.	EXPEDITION	Journey or voyage made for a specific purpose
46.	FILTERING	Slipping through slowly as if through an obstruction
47.	FLUTTERED	Waved or flapped about
48.	FRINGES	At the outer edges or border
49.	FUTILE	Incapable of producing any result

Mrs. Frisby Vocabulary Word List Cont.

No.	Word	Clue/Definition
50.	GALE	A very strong wind
51.	GRAVELY	Seriously; solemnly
52.	HARROW	Agricultural implement with teeth or upright disks, for leveling and breaking up dirt clods
53.	HERMIT	Any person living in seclusion
54.	HESITATED	Was reluctant or waited to act because of fear or indecision
55.	HYPODERMIC	Syringe or needle that injects medicine under the skin
56.	ILLUSION	Something that deceives by producing a false impression of reality
57.	IMPASSE	Situation offering no escape
58.	INCINERATOR	Furnace or apparatus for burning materials
59.	INCLINE	Upward slant
60.	INCURRING	Bringing upon oneself
61.	INDIGNANTLY	In a manner expressing great anger or scorn
62.	INEXORABLE	Such that cannot be moved or influenced by persuasion
63.	INEXTRICABLY	In a manner incapable of being disentangled
64.	INKLING	Vague idea or notion
65.	INLAID	Mounted into and flush with the surface of an object
66.	IRRELEVANTLY	In a manner not having anything to do with the matter at hand
67.	MANIPULATED	Worked, operated, or treated with the hands
68.	PARTITIONS	Dividers
69.	PEDDLER	Person who goes from place to place selling small articles
70.	PERSPIRATION	Sweat
71.	PESSIMIST	Person who sees everything in a negative or the worst possible way
72.	PLAINTIVE	Expressing sorrow or melancholy
73.	PLEAD	Make an earnest request
74.	PROSPECT	Outlook for the future
75.	PROTRUDED	Stuck out; extended beyond
76.	RECESSED	Set back
77.	RESPITE	A break
78.	ROVING	Wandering about; going from place to place
79.	SATCHEL	Small bag, sometimes with a shoulder strap
80.	SCARCE	Insufficient to satisfy the need or demand
81.	SCURRIED	Scampered or ran hastily
82.	SENTRY	Guard; watch
83.	SHINNY	Climb by using both hands and legs for gripping
84.	SILOS	Airtight pits or towers in which fodder is stored
85.	SKEPTICAL	Doubtful; not easily persuaded or convinced
86.	SPINY	Covered with thorns or prickles
87.	STOCKY	Having a sturdy form or build
88.	SUBDUED	Quieted; less active than usual
89.	TOILING	Working with exhausting labor or effort
90.	TREMBLING	Shaking involuntarily with quick, short movements as from fear, excitement, or cold
91.	TWINED	Interwoven; wrapped around
92.	UNERRINGLY	Without mistakes
93.	VACANT	Empty
94.	VANTAGE	Position that provides a clear, broad view
95.	VENTILATION	System that circulates air

Mrs. Frisby Vocabulary Word List Cont.

No.	Word	Clue/Definition
96.	VENTURED	Dared to do something dangerous or risky
97.	VIGOROUS	Strong; active; robust
98.	WEARILY	In a tired or worn-out manner
99.	WRITHING	Making twisting or turning movements
100	YIELDED	Gave way

1. Side by side; beside each other in a line

2. A break

3. Prepared for growing crops; tended; nurtured

4. Courteous; gracious; friendly

5. In a manner feeling or showing hopelessness

6. The outline of a figure, mass, land, etc.

7. Filled with sudden, overpowering surprise or wonder

8. Vague idea or notion

9. Shaking involuntarily with quick, short movements as from fear, excitement, or cold

10. Making a continuous, low, monotonous sound

11. Suspended (a meeting) until a later time or another place

12. Came together to meet at a point or in a line

13. Dissatisfaction; a restless desire for something more

14. System that circulates air

15. Airtight pits or towers in which fodder is stored

16. The condition of being completely puzzled

17. Sent off on a specific errand

18. Such that cannot be moved or influenced by persuasion

19. Climb by using both hands and legs for gripping

20. Suddenly or unexpectedly

Mrs. Frisby and the Rats of NIMH Vocabulary Fill In The Blanks 1 Answer Key

ABREAST

1. Side by side; beside each other in a line

RESPITE

2. A break

CULTIVATED

3. Prepared for growing crops; tended; nurtured

CORDIAL

4. Courteous; gracious; friendly

DESPAIRINGLY

5. In a manner feeling or showing hopelessness

CONTOUR

6. The outline of a figure, mass, land, etc.

ASTONISHED

7. Filled with sudden, overpowering surprise or wonder

INKLING

8. Vague idea or notion

TREMBLING

9. Shaking involuntarily with quick, short movements as from fear, excitement, or cold

DRONING

10. Making a continuous, low, monotonous sound

ADJOURNED

11. Suspended (a meeting) until a later time or another place

CONVERGED

12. Came together to meet at a point or in a line

DISCONTENT

13. Dissatisfaction; a restless desire for something more

VENTILATION

14. System that circulates air

SILOS

15. Airtight pits or towers in which fodder is stored

BEWILDERMENT

16. The condition of being completely puzzled

DISPATCHED

17. Sent off on a specific errand

INEXORABLE

18. Such that cannot be moved or influenced by persuasion

SHINNY

19. Climb by using both hands and legs for gripping

ABRUPTLY

20. Suddenly or unexpectedly

1. Interwoven; wrapped around

2. Stuck out; extended beyond

3. Spoken or read aloud to be written or recorded

4. Imperfect; faulty

5. Covered with thorns or prickles

6. Strainer; a perforated pan used for draining liquids

7. Slipping through slowly as if through an obstruction

8. Gave way

9. Listen secretly to a private conversation

10. Waved or flapped about

11. Containing too many things, often unorganized

12. Prepared for growing crops; tended; nurtured

13. In a manner not having anything to do with the matter at hand

14. Came forth

15. Bringing upon oneself

16. Dissatisfaction; a restless desire for something more

17. The moving from a higher to a lower place

18. Upward slant

19. Having or showing a clever or shrewd mind

20. In a manner feeling or showing hopelessness

Mrs. Frisby and the Rats of NIMH Vocabulary Fill In The Blanks 2 Answer Key

TWINED

1. Interwoven; wrapped around

PROTRUDED

2. Stuck out; extended beyond

DICTATED

3. Spoken or read aloud to be written or recorded

DEFECTIVE

4. Imperfect; faulty

SPINY

5. Covered with thorns or prickles

COLANDER

6. Strainer; a perforated pan used for draining liquids

FILTERING

7. Slipping through slowly as if through an obstruction

YIELDED

8. Gave way

EAVESDROP

9. Listen secretly to a private conversation

FLUTTERED

10. Waved or flapped about

CLUTTERED

11. Containing too many things, often unorganized

CULTIVATED

12. Prepared for growing crops; tended; nurtured

IRRELEVANTLY

13. In a manner not having anything to do with the matter at hand

EMERGED

14. Came forth

INCURRING

15. Bringing upon oneself

DISCONTENT

16. Dissatisfaction; a restless desire for something more

DESCENT

17. The moving from a higher to a lower place

INCLINE

18. Upward slant

ASTUTE

19. Having or showing a clever or shrewd mind

DESPAIRINGLY

20. In a manner feeling or showing hopelessness

Mrs. Frisby and the Rats of NIMH Vocabulary Fill In The Blanks 3

1. Prevalent and spreading rapidly among many individuals

2. Airtight pits or towers in which fodder is stored

3. System that circulates air

4. Make an earnest request

5. Believing that people are only motivated by selfishness

6. In a manner feeling or showing hopelessness

7. Any person living in seclusion

8. Was reluctant or waited to act because of fear or indecision

9. Dared to do something dangerous or risky

10. Worked, operated, or treated with the hands

11. The outline of a figure, mass, land, etc.

12. Imprisonment

13. Terribly

14. Outlook for the future

15. Discuss

16. Made by human work or art, not by nature

17. Troubled or nervous

18. Climb by using both hands and legs for gripping

19. In a manner incapable of being disentangled

20. Dissatisfaction; a restless desire for something more

Mrs. Frisby and the Rats of NIMH Vocabulary Fill In The Blanks 3 Answer Key

EPIDEMIC   1. Prevalent and spreading rapidly among many individuals

SILOS   2. Airtight pits or towers in which fodder is stored

VENTILATION   3. System that circulates air

PLEAD   4. Make an earnest request

CYNICAL   5. Believing that people are only motivated by selfishness

DESPAIRINGLY   6. In a manner feeling or showing hopelessness

HERMIT   7. Any person living in seclusion

HESITATED   8. Was reluctant or waited to act because of fear or indecision

VENTURED   9. Dared to do something dangerous or risky

MANIPULATED   10. Worked, operated, or treated with the hands

CONTOUR   11. The outline of a figure, mass, land, etc.

CAPTIVITY   12. Imprisonment

DREADFULLY   13. Terribly

PROSPECT   14. Outlook for the future

CONFER   15. Discuss

ARTIFICIAL   16. Made by human work or art, not by nature

AGITATED   17. Troubled or nervous

SHINNY   18. Climb by using both hands and legs for gripping

INEXTRICABLY   19. In a manner incapable of being disentangled

DISCONTENT   20. Dissatisfaction; a restless desire for something more

1. Overhanging edges of a roof

2. Waved or flapped about

3. Covered with thorns or prickles

4. Wandering about; going from place to place

5. Sent off on a specific errand

6. In a manner not having anything to do with the matter at hand

7. Agricultural implement with teeth or upright disks, for leveling and breaking up dirt clods

8. Terribly

9. Guard; watch

10. Dared to do something dangerous or risky

11. Situation offering no escape

12. Discuss

13. The outline of a figure, mass, land, etc.

14. Passageway giving access to rooms, apartments, etc.

15. Scampered or ran hastily

16. In a manner incapable of being disentangled

17. Sweat

18. Position that provides a clear, broad view

19. System that circulates air

20. Shaking involuntarily with quick, short movements as from fear, excitement, or cold

Mrs. Frisby and the Rats of NIMH Vocabulary Fill In The Blanks 4 Answer Key

EAVES

1. Overhanging edges of a roof

FLUTTERED

2. Waved or flapped about

SPINY

3. Covered with thorns or prickles

ROVING

4. Wandering about; going from place to place

DISPATCHED

5. Sent off on a specific errand

IRRELEVANTLY

6. In a manner not having anything to do with the matter at hand

HARROW

7. Agricultural implement with teeth or upright disks, for leveling and breaking up dirt clods

DREADFULLY

8. Terribly

SENTRY

9. Guard; watch

VENTURED

10. Dared to do something dangerous or risky

IMPASSE

11. Situation offering no escape

CONFER

12. Discuss

CONTOUR

13. The outline of a figure, mass, land, etc.

CORRIDOR

14. Passageway giving access to rooms, apartments, etc.

SCURRIED

15. Scampered or ran hastily

INEXTRICABLY

16. In a manner incapable of being disentangled

PERSPIRATION

17. Sweat

VANTAGE

18. Position that provides a clear, broad view

VENTILATION

19. System that circulates air

TREMBLING

20. Shaking involuntarily with quick, short movements as from fear, excitement, or cold

Mrs. Frisby and the Rats of NIMH Vocabulary Matching 1

___ 1. DRONING   A. In a manner feeling or showing hopelessness

___ 2. CORRIDOR   B. Imperfect; faulty

___ 3. CURSORY   C. Came forth

___ 4. COMPILED   D. Empty

___ 5. HYPODERMIC   E. Passageway giving access to rooms, apartments, etc.

___ 6. HERMIT   F. Sent off on a specific errand

___ 7. CONVERGED   G. Agricultural implement with teeth or upright disks, for
                           leveling and breaking up dirt clods

___ 8. EMERGED   H. Making a continuous, low, monotonous sound

___ 9. DEFECTIVE   I. Came together to meet at a point or in a line

___10. SHINNY   J. System that circulates air

___11. VENTILATION   K. Situation offering no escape

___12. UNERRINGLY   L. Position that provides a clear, broad view

___13. VANTAGE   M. Without mistakes

___14. YIELDED   N. Furnace or apparatus for burning materials

___15. DISPATCHED   O. Bringing upon oneself

___16. EPIDEMIC   P. Syringe or needle that injects medicine under the skin

___17. EXPEDITION   Q. Discuss

___18. VACANT   R. Any person living in seclusion

___19. INCURRING   S. Journey or voyage made for a specific purpose

___20. FILTERING   T. Slipping through slowly as if through an obstruction

___21. HARROW   U. Gave way

___22. CONFER   V. Prevalent and spreading rapidly among many individuals

___23. IMPASSE   W. Made of materials from various sources

___24. INCINERATOR   X. Performed rapidly with little attention to detail

___25. DESPAIRINGLY   Y. Climb by using both hands and legs for gripping

Mrs. Frisby and the Rats of NIMH Vocabulary Matching 1 Answer Key

H - 1. DRONING

E - 2. CORRIDOR

X - 3. CURSORY

W - 4. COMPILED

P - 5. HYPODERMIC

R - 6. HERMIT

I - 7. CONVERGED

C - 8. EMERGED

B - 9. DEFECTIVE

Y - 10. SHINNY

J - 11. VENTILATION

M - 12. UNERRINGLY

L - 13. VANTAGE

U - 14. YIELDED

F - 15. DISPATCHED

V - 16. EPIDEMIC

S - 17. EXPEDITION

D - 18. VACANT

O - 19. INCURRING

T - 20. FILTERING

G - 21. HARROW

Q - 22. CONFER

K - 23. IMPASSE

N - 24. INCINERATOR

A - 25. DESPAIRINGLY

A. In a manner feeling or showing hopelessness

B. Imperfect; faulty

C. Came forth

D. Empty

E. Passageway giving access to rooms, apartments, etc.

F. Sent off on a specific errand

G. Agricultural implement with teeth or upright disks, for leveling and breaking up dirt clods

H. Making a continuous, low, monotonous sound

I. Came together to meet at a point or in a line

J. System that circulates air

K. Situation offering no escape

L. Position that provides a clear, broad view

M. Without mistakes

N. Furnace or apparatus for burning materials

O. Bringing upon oneself

P. Syringe or needle that injects medicine under the skin

Q. Discuss

R. Any person living in seclusion

S. Journey or voyage made for a specific purpose

T. Slipping through slowly as if through an obstruction

U. Gave way

V. Prevalent and spreading rapidly among many individuals

W. Made of materials from various sources

X. Performed rapidly with little attention to detail

Y. Climb by using both hands and legs for gripping

Mrs. Frisby and the Rats of NIMH Vocabulary Matching 2

___ 1. SUBDUED	A. Mounted into and flush with the surface of an object
___ 2. FILTERING	B. Quieted; less active than usual
___ 3. HARROW	C. Believing that people are only motivated by selfishness
___ 4. VANTAGE	D. Imprisonment
___ 5. WEARILY	E. In a tired or worn-out manner
___ 6. EXERT	F. Sweat
___ 7. DESCENT	G. Syringe or needle that injects medicine under the skin
___ 8. FRINGES	H. A very strong wind
___ 9. PROSPECT	I. Imperfect; faulty
___10. PLEAD	J. At the outer edges or border
___11. AUTHORITATIVELY	K. In a manner incapable of being disentangled
___12. TWINED	L. Interwoven; wrapped around
___13. INLAID	M. Vague idea or notion
___14. ASTONISHED	N. In a commanding way
___15. GALE	O. Agricultural implement with teeth or upright disks, for leveling and breaking up dirt clods
___16. HYPODERMIC	P. Outlook for the future
___17. DEFECTIVE	Q. Put forth or use energetically
___18. INEXORABLE	R. Make an earnest request
___19. CAPTIVITY	S. The moving from a higher to a lower place
___20. EMERGED	T. Filled with sudden, overpowering surprise or wonder
___21. INEXTRICABLY	U. Such that cannot be moved or influenced by persuasion
___22. CYNICAL	V. Position that provides a clear, broad view
___23. PERSPIRATION	W. Listen secretly to a private conversation
___24. INKLING	X. Came forth
___25. EAVESDROP	Y. Slipping through slowly as if through an obstruction

Mrs. Frisby and the Rats of NIMH Vocabulary Matching 2 Answer Key

B - 1. SUBDUED

A. Mounted into and flush with the surface of an object

Y - 2. FILTERING

B. Quieted; less active than usual

O - 3. HARROW

C. Believing that people are only motivated by selfishness

V - 4. VANTAGE

D. Imprisonment

E - 5. WEARILY

E. In a tired or worn-out manner

Q - 6. EXERT

F. Sweat

S - 7. DESCENT

G. Syringe or needle that injects medicine under the skin

J - 8. FRINGES

H. A very strong wind

P - 9. PROSPECT

I. Imperfect; faulty

R -10. PLEAD

J. At the outer edges or border

N -11. AUTHORITATIVELY

K. In a manner incapable of being disentangled

L - 12. TWINED

L. Interwoven; wrapped around

A -13. INLAID

M. Vague idea or notion

T - 14. ASTONISHED

N. In a commanding way

H -15. GALE

O. Agricultural implement with teeth or upright disks, for leveling and breaking up dirt clods

G -16. HYPODERMIC

P. Outlook for the future

I - 17. DEFECTIVE

Q. Put forth or use energetically

U -18. INEXORABLE

R. Make an earnest request

D -19. CAPTIVITY

S. The moving from a higher to a lower place

X -20. EMERGED

T. Filled with sudden, overpowering surprise or wonder

K -21. INEXTRICABLY

U. Such that cannot be moved or influenced by persuasion

C -22. CYNICAL

V. Position that provides a clear, broad view

F -23. PERSPIRATION

W. Listen secretly to a private conversation

M -24. INKLING

X. Came forth

W -25. EAVESDROP

Y. Slipping through slowly as if through an obstruction

Mrs. Frisby and the Rats of NIMH Vocabulary Matching 3

___ 1. CIRCUMSTANCES

___ 2. TWINED

___ 3. ADMONISHED

___ 4. MANIPULATED

___ 5. ILLUSION

___ 6. PESSIMIST

___ 7. CULTIVATED

___ 8. PLEAD

___ 9. COMRADESHIP

___10. VENTILATION

___11. WRITHING

___12. DISCONTENT

___13. DESCENT

___14. ARTIFICIAL

___15. PARTITIONS

___16. TREMBLING

___17. PROTRUDED

___18. FRINGES

___19. VIGOROUS

___20. INEXORABLE

___21. SPINY

___22. FUTILE

___23. INCURRING

___24. CURSORY

___25. VANTAGE

A. Made by human work or art, not by nature

B. Stuck out; extended beyond

C. The moving from a higher to a lower place

D. Friendship; companionship

E. Covered with thorns or prickles

F. Dissatisfaction; a restless desire for something more

G. Mildly scolded; spoken to in disapproval

H. Interwoven; wrapped around

I. System that circulates air

J. Position that provides a clear, broad view

K. Something that deceives by producing a false impression of reality

L. Such that cannot be moved or influenced by persuasion

M. At the outer edges or border

N. Dividers

O. Worked, operated, or treated with the hands

P. Bringing upon oneself

Q. Incapable of producing any result

R. Strong; active; robust

S. Making twisting or turning movements

T. Prepared for growing crops; tended; nurtured

U. Make an earnest request

V. Shaking involuntarily with quick, short movements as from fear, excitement, or cold

W. Person who sees everything in a negative or the worst possible way

X. Performed rapidly with little attention to detail

Y. Conditions surrounding an event

Mrs. Frisby and the Rats of NIMH Vocabulary Matching 3 Answer Key

Y - 1. CIRCUMSTANCES

H - 2. TWINED

G - 3. ADMONISHED

O - 4. MANIPULATED

K - 5. ILLUSION

W - 6. PESSIMIST

T - 7. CULTIVATED

U - 8. PLEAD

D - 9. COMRADESHIP

I - 10. VENTILATION

S - 11. WRITHING

F - 12. DISCONTENT

C - 13. DESCENT

A - 14. ARTIFICIAL

N - 15. PARTITIONS

V - 16. TREMBLING

B - 17. PROTRUDED

M - 18. FRINGES

R - 19. VIGOROUS

L - 20. INEXORABLE

E - 21. SPINY

Q - 22. FUTILE

P - 23. INCURRING

X - 24. CURSORY

J - 25. VANTAGE

A. Made by human work or art, not by nature

B. Stuck out; extended beyond

C. The moving from a higher to a lower place

D. Friendship; companionship

E. Covered with thorns or prickles

F. Dissatisfaction; a restless desire for something more

G. Mildly scolded; spoken to in disapproval

H. Interwoven; wrapped around

I. System that circulates air

J. Position that provides a clear, broad view

K. Something that deceives by producing a false impression of reality

L. Such that cannot be moved or influenced by persuasion

M. At the outer edges or border

N. Dividers

O. Worked, operated, or treated with the hands

P. Bringing upon oneself

Q. Incapable of producing any result

R. Strong; active; robust

S. Making twisting or turning movements

T. Prepared for growing crops; tended; nurtured

U. Make an earnest request

V. Shaking involuntarily with quick, short movements as from fear, excitement, or cold

W. Person who sees everything in a negative or the worst possible way

X. Performed rapidly with little attention to detail

Y. Conditions surrounding an event

Mrs. Frisby and the Rats of NIMH Vocabulary Matching 4

___ 1. INCURRING

___ 2. ELEGANTLY

___ 3. DRONING

___ 4. EXERT

___ 5. TOILING

___ 6. INEXTRICABLY

___ 7. HERMIT

___ 8. ARTIFICIAL

___ 9. ROVING

___10. INLAID

___11. SATCHEL

___12. UNERRINGLY

___13. GRAVELY

___14. EXPEDITION

___15. INKLING

___16. ADJOURNED

___17. HARROW

___18. CLUTTERED

___19. WRITHING

___20. STOCKY

___21. VACANT

___22. INCINERATOR

___23. BEWILDERMENT

___24. SENTRY

___25. DELIBERATELY

A. Without mistakes

B. In a manner incapable of being disentangled

C. Made by human work or art, not by nature

D. Empty

E. Working with exhausting labor or effort

F. Put forth or use energetically

G. Suspended (a meeting) until a later time or another place

H. Vague idea or notion

I. The condition of being completely puzzled

J. Seriously; solemnly

K. Furnace or apparatus for burning materials

L. Having a sturdy form or build

M. Bringing upon oneself

N. Guard; watch

O. Wandering about; going from place to place

P. Any person living in seclusion

Q. Small bag, sometimes with a shoulder strap

R. Mounted into and flush with the surface of an object

S. Containing too many things, often unorganized

T. Making a continuous, low, monotonous sound

U. Agricultural implement with teeth or upright disks, for leveling and breaking up dirt clods

V. Making twisting or turning movements

W. In a splendid or luxurious style or design

X. Intentionally; on purpose; with forethought

Y. Journey or voyage made for a specific purpose

Mrs. Frisby and the Rats of NIMH Vocabulary Matching 4 Answer Key

M - 1. INCURRING

W - 2. ELEGANTLY

T - 3. DRONING

F - 4. EXERT

E - 5. TOILING

B - 6. INEXTRICABLY

P - 7. HERMIT

C - 8. ARTIFICIAL

O - 9. ROVING

R -10. INLAID

Q -11. SATCHEL

A -12. UNERRINGLY

J - 13. GRAVELY

Y -14. EXPEDITION

H -15. INKLING

G -16. ADJOURNED

U -17. HARROW

S -18. CLUTTERED

V -19. WRITHING

L - 20. STOCKY

D -21. VACANT

K -22. INCINERATOR

I - 23. BEWILDERMENT

N -24. SENTRY

X -25. DELIBERATELY

A. Without mistakes

B. In a manner incapable of being disentangled

C. Made by human work or art, not by nature

D. Empty

E. Working with exhausting labor or effort

F. Put forth or use energetically

G. Suspended (a meeting) until a later time or another place

H. Vague idea or notion

I. The condition of being completely puzzled

J. Seriously; solemnly

K. Furnace or apparatus for burning materials

L. Having a sturdy form or build

M. Bringing upon oneself

N. Guard; watch

O. Wandering about; going from place to place

P. Any person living in seclusion

Q. Small bag, sometimes with a shoulder strap

R. Mounted into and flush with the surface of an object

S. Containing too many things, often unorganized

T. Making a continuous, low, monotonous sound

U. Agricultural implement with teeth or upright disks, for leveling and breaking up dirt clods

V. Making twisting or turning movements

W. In a splendid or luxurious style or design

X. Intentionally; on purpose; with forethought

Y. Journey or voyage made for a specific purpose

Mrs. Frisby and the Rats of NIMH Vocabulary Magic Squares 1

Match the definition with the vocabulary word. Put your answers in the magic squares below. When your answers are correct, all columns and rows will add to the same number.

A. DICTATED
B. INCURRING
C. CONCEALED
D. VIGOROUS
E. DESCENT
F. WEARILY

G. DELIBERATELY
H. CIRCUMSTANCES
I. PEDDLER
J. SHINNY
K. DREADFULLY
L. GRAVELY

M. INKLING
N. INCLINE
O. CURSORY
P. INCINERATOR

1. Hidden
2. Climb by using both hands and legs for gripping
3. In a tired or worn-out manner
4. Performed rapidly with little attention to detail
5. Furnace or apparatus for burning materials
6. The moving from a higher to a lower place
7. Person who goes from place to place selling small articles
8. Strong; active; robust

9. Vague idea or notion
10. Conditions surrounding an event
11. Seriously; solemnly
12. Spoken or read aloud to be written or recorded
13. Bringing upon oneself
14. Terribly
15. Intentionally; on purpose; with forethought
16. Upward slant

A=	B=	C=	D=
E=	F=	G=	H=
I=	J=	K=	L=
M=	N=	O=	P=

Mrs. Frisby and the Rats of NIMH Vocabulary Magic Squares 1 Answer Key

Match the definition with the vocabulary word. Put your answers in the magic squares below. When your answers are correct, all columns and rows will add to the same number.

A. DICTATED
B. INCURRING
C. CONCEALED
D. VIGOROUS
E. DESCENT
F. WEARILY

G. DELIBERATELY
H. CIRCUMSTANCES
I. PEDDLER
J. SHINNY
K. DREADFULLY
L. GRAVELY

M. INKLING
N. INCLINE
O. CURSORY
P. INCINERATOR

1. Hidden
2. Climb by using both hands and legs for gripping
3. In a tired or worn-out manner
4. Performed rapidly with little attention to detail
5. Furnace or apparatus for burning materials
6. The moving from a higher to a lower place
7. Person who goes from place to place selling small articles
8. Strong; active; robust
9. Vague idea or notion
10. Conditions surrounding an event
11. Seriously; solemnly
12. Spoken or read aloud to be written or recorded
13. Bringing upon oneself
14. Terribly
15. Intentionally; on purpose; with forethought
16. Upward slant

A=12	B=13	C=1	D=8
E=6	F=3	G=15	H=10
I=7	J=2	K=14	L=11
M=9	N=16	O=4	P=5

Mrs. Frisby and the Rats of NIMH Vocabulary Magic Squares 2

Match the definition with the vocabulary word. Put your answers in the magic squares below. When your answers are correct, all columns and rows will add to the same number.

A. INCINERATOR
B. FILTERING
C. TWINED
D. PESSIMIST
E. INCURRING
F. EXPEDITION

G. FRINGES
H. WRITHING
I. SATCHEL
J. COMPILED
K. CLUTTERED
L. DEBRIS

M. EXERT
N. CONFER
O. STOCKY
P. CONTOUR

1. Slipping through slowly as if through an obstruction
2. At the outer edges or border
3. Containing too many things, often unorganized
4. Discuss
5. Put forth or use energetically
6. Bits and pieces of rubbish; litter
7. Making twisting or turning movements
8. Furnace or apparatus for burning materials
9. The outline of a figure, mass, land, etc.
10. Small bag, sometimes with a shoulder strap
11. Bringing upon oneself
12. Person who sees everything in a negative or the worst possible way
13. Interwoven; wrapped around
14. Journey or voyage made for a specific purpose
15. Made of materials from various sources
16. Having a sturdy form or build

A=	B=	C=	D=
E=	F=	G=	H=
I=	J=	K=	L=
M=	N=	O=	P=

Mrs. Frisby and the Rats of NIMH Vocabulary Magic Squares 2 Answer Key

Match the definition with the vocabulary word. Put your answers in the magic squares below. When your answers are correct, all columns and rows will add to the same number.

A. INCINERATOR
B. FILTERING
C. TWINED
D. PESSIMIST
E. INCURRING
F. EXPEDITION

G. FRINGES
H. WRITHING
I. SATCHEL
J. COMPILED
K. CLUTTERED
L. DEBRIS

M. EXERT
N. CONFER
O. STOCKY
P. CONTOUR

1. Slipping through slowly as if through an obstruction
2. At the outer edges or border
3. Containing too many things, often unorganized
4. Discuss
5. Put forth or use energetically
6. Bits and pieces of rubbish; litter
7. Making twisting or turning movements
8. Furnace or apparatus for burning materials
9. The outline of a figure, mass, land, etc.
10. Small bag, sometimes with a shoulder strap
11. Bringing upon oneself
12. Person who sees everything in a negative or the worst possible way
13. Interwoven; wrapped around
14. Journey or voyage made for a specific purpose
15. Made of materials from various sources
16. Having a sturdy form or build

A=8	B=1	C=13	D=12
E=11	F=14	G=2	H=7
I=10	J=15	K=3	L=6
M=5	N=4	O=16	P=9

Mrs. Frisby and the Rats of NIMH Vocabulary Magic Squares 3

Match the definition with the vocabulary word. Put your answers in the magic squares below. When your answers are correct, all columns and rows will add to the same number.

A. PROTRUDED
B. PLAINTIVE
C. CIRCUMSTANCES
D. HYPODERMIC
E. PEDDLER
F. DISCONTENT

G. VACANT
H. CONVERGED
I. INKLING
J. CAPTIVITY
K. TREMBLING
L. CULTIVATED

M. STOCKY
N. FILTERING
O. FLUTTERED
P. HERMIT

1. Stuck out; extended beyond
2. Slipping through slowly as if through an obstruction
3. Imprisonment
4. Person who goes from place to place selling small articles
5. Empty
6. Prepared for growing crops; tended; nurtured
7. Any person living in seclusion
8. Conditions surrounding an event
9. Waved or flapped about
10. Syringe or needle that injects medicine under the skin
11. Came together to meet at a point or in a line
12. Shaking involuntarily with quick, short movements as from fear, excitement, or cold
13. Vague idea or notion
14. Dissatisfaction; a restless desire for something more
15. Expressing sorrow or melancholy
16. Having a sturdy form or build

A=	B=	C=	D=
E=	F=	G=	H=
I=	J=	K=	L=
M=	N=	O=	P=

Mrs. Frisby and the Rats of NIMH Vocabulary Magic Squares 3 Answer Key

Match the definition with the vocabulary word. Put your answers in the magic squares below. When your answers are correct, all columns and rows will add to the same number.

A. PROTRUDED
B. PLAINTIVE
C. CIRCUMSTANCES
D. HYPODERMIC
E. PEDDLER
F. DISCONTENT

G. VACANT
H. CONVERGED
I. INKLING
J. CAPTIVITY
K. TREMBLING
L. CULTIVATED

M. STOCKY
N. FILTERING
O. FLUTTERED
P. HERMIT

1. Stuck out; extended beyond
2. Slipping through slowly as if through an obstruction
3. Imprisonment
4. Person who goes from place to place selling small articles
5. Empty
6. Prepared for growing crops; tended; nurtured
7. Any person living in seclusion
8. Conditions surrounding an event
9. Waved or flapped about
10. Syringe or needle that injects medicine under the skin
11. Came together to meet at a point or in a line
12. Shaking involuntarily with quick, short movements as from fear, excitement, or cold
13. Vague idea or notion
14. Dissatisfaction; a restless desire for something more
15. Expressing sorrow or melancholy
16. Having a sturdy form or build

A=1	B=15	C=8	D=10
E=4	F=14	G=5	H=11
I=13	J=3	K=12	L=6
M=16	N=2	O=9	P=7

Mrs. Frisby and the Rats of NIMH Vocabulary Magic Squares 4

Match the definition with the vocabulary word. Put your answers in the magic squares below. When your answers are correct, all columns and rows will add to the same number.

A. ILLUSION
B. IMPASSE
C. HESITATED
D. YIELDED
E. UNERRINGLY
F. DESPAIRINGLY

G. ADJOURNED
H. VENTILATION
I. MANIPULATED
J. INKLING
K. ADMONISHED
L. FRINGES

M. SILOS
N. HYPODERMIC
O. ELEGANTLY
P. WRITHING

1. In a splendid or luxurious style or design
2. Gave way
3. Vague idea or notion
4. Without mistakes
5. Worked, operated, or treated with the hands
6. In a manner feeling or showing hopelessness
7. Making twisting or turning movements
8. Was reluctant or waited to act because of fear or indecision
9. System that circulates air
10. Mildly scolded; spoken to in disapproval
11. Something that deceives by producing a false impression of reality
12. Syringe or needle that injects medicine under the skin
13. Situation offering no escape
14. Airtight pits or towers in which fodder is stored
15. Suspended (a meeting) until a later time or another place
16. At the outer edges or border

A=	B=	C=	D=
E=	F=	G=	H=
I=	J=	K=	L=
M=	N=	O=	P=

Mrs. Frisby and the Rats of NIMH Vocabulary Magic Squares 4 Answer Key

Match the definition with the vocabulary word. Put your answers in the magic squares below. When your answers are correct, all columns and rows will add to the same number.

A. ILLUSION
B. IMPASSE
C. HESITATED
D. YIELDED
E. UNERRINGLY
F. DESPAIRINGLY

G. ADJOURNED
H. VENTILATION
I. MANIPULATED
J. INKLING
K. ADMONISHED
L. FRINGES

M. SILOS
N. HYPODERMIC
O. ELEGANTLY
P. WRITHING

1. In a splendid or luxurious style or design
2. Gave way
3. Vague idea or notion
4. Without mistakes
5. Worked, operated, or treated with the hands
6. In a manner feeling or showing hopelessness
7. Making twisting or turning movements
8. Was reluctant or waited to act because of fear or indecision
9. System that circulates air
10. Mildly scolded; spoken to in disapproval
11. Something that deceives by producing a false impression of reality
12. Syringe or needle that injects medicine under the skin
13. Situation offering no escape
14. Airtight pits or towers in which fodder is stored
15. Suspended (a meeting) until a later time or another place
16. At the outer edges or border

A=11	B=13	C=8	D=2
E=4	F=6	G=15	H=9
I=5	J=3	K=10	L=16
M=14	N=12	O=1	P=7

```
C  A  S  T  O  N  I  S  H  E  D  I  N  C  L  I  N  E  D  N
V  A  C  A  N  T  W  C  F  S  U  B  D  U  E  D  E  A  S  K
Q  S  P  I  N  Y  R  R  O  V  I  N  V  W  W  X  E  A  E  H
E  L  I  T  U  F  I  M  D  N  G  F  O  D  E  L  B  S  N  G
J  Y  H  I  I  N  T  H  L  W  F  R  T  R  P  R  Y  C  T  N
B  D  I  N  G  V  H  A  N  E  R  E  T  E  E  R  L  V  R  W
D  E  F  E  C  T  I  V  E  A  U  G  R  A  V  E  L  Y  Y  W
R  S  S  X  L  D  N  T  H  R  O  S  S  D  I  H  A  L  R  F
E  P  C  T  P  D  G  R  Y  I  T  T  E  F  T  Y  C  T  O  C
S  A  O  R  R  I  E  J  H  L  N  O  V  U  N  P  I  N  V  J
P  I  N  I  O  N  T  D  E  Y  O  C  A  L  I  O  T  A  I  H
I  R  C  C  T  K  U  E  R  A  C  K  E  L  A  D  P  V  N  H
T  I  E  A  R  L  T  L  M  S  V  Y  X  Y  L  E  Y  E  G  L
E  N  A  B  U  I  S  I  I  I  C  E  G  K  P  R  R  L  T  F
M  G  L  L  D  N  A  P  T  R  Q  A  S  G  F  M  C  E  W  R
N  L  E  Y  E  G  Y  M  G  B  L  U  R  D  S  I  Q  R  I  D
W  Y  D  C  D  G  B  O  N  E  D  V  Y  C  R  C  R  R  N  B
T  T  D  E  T  A  T  C  I  D  X  B  T  X  E  O  J  I  E  Q
C  O  L  A  N  D  E  R  E  T  T  U  L  C  R  F  P  D  D  H
```

A break (7)

A very strong wind (4)

Agricultural implement with teeth or upright disks, for leveling and breaking up dirt clods (6)

Any person living in seclusion (6)

At the outer edges or border (7)

Bits and pieces of rubbish; litter (6)

Containing too many things, often unorganized (9)

Covered with thorns or prickles (5)

Discuss (6)

Empty (6)

Expressing sorrow or melancholy (9)

Filled with sudden, overpowering surprise or wonder (10)

Gave way (7)

Guard; watch (6)

Having a sturdy form or build (6)

Having or showing a clever or shrewd mind (6)

Hidden (9)

Imperfect; faulty (9)

Imprisonment (9)

In a manner feeling or showing hopelessness (12)

In a manner incapable of being disentangled (12)

In a manner not having anything to do with the matter at hand (12)

In a manner that is mysterious or obscure in meaning (11)

In a tired or worn-out manner (7)

Incapable of producing any result (6)

Insufficient to satisfy the need or demand (6)

Interwoven; wrapped around (6)

Listen secretly to a private conversation (9)

Made of materials from various sources (8)

Make an earnest request (5)

Making twisting or turning movements (8)

Mounted into and flush with the surface of an object (6)

Overhanging edges of a roof (5)

Period of partial darkness between day and night as the sun begins to set (4)

Put forth or use energetically (5)

Quieted; less active than usual (7)

Seriously; solemnly (7)

Side by side; beside each other in a line (7)

Spoken or read aloud to be written or recorded (8)

Strainer; a perforated pan used for draining liquids (8)

Stuck out; extended beyond (9)

Syringe or needle that injects medicine under the skin (10)

Terribly (10)

The outline of a figure, mass, land, etc. (7)

Upward slant (7)

Vague idea or notion (7)

Wandering about; going from place to place (6)

```
C A S T O N I S H E D I N C L I N E D
V A C A N T W C F S U B D U E D E A S
  S P I N Y R R O   I     W   X E A   E
E L I T U F I     N   O D E L B     N
  Y   I   I N T     L W F R R P R Y T
  D I N G V H A   E R E T E E L     R
D E F E C T I V E A U G R A V E L Y Y
R S S X L D N T H R O S S D I H A L R
E P C T P D G   Y I T T E F T Y C T O
S A O R R I E   H L N O V U N P I N V
P I N I O N T D E Y O C A L I O T A I
I R C C T K U E R A C K E L A D P V N
T I E A R L T L M S V Y Y L E Y E G
E N A B U I S I I I C E G K P R R L T
  G L L D N A P T R   A S     M C E W
  L E Y E G   M   B L U R D   I R I
  Y D D   O   E D       C R C     R N
    D E T A T C I D         C   R C I E
C O L A N D E R E T T U L C       P   D
```

A break (7)	Incapable of producing any result (6)

A break (7)

A very strong wind (4)

Agricultural implement with teeth or upright disks, for leveling and breaking up dirt clods (6)

Any person living in seclusion (6)

At the outer edges or border (7)

Bits and pieces of rubbish; litter (6)

Containing too many things, often unorganized (9)

Covered with thorns or prickles (5)

Discuss (6)

Empty (6)

Expressing sorrow or melancholy (9)

Filled with sudden, overpowering surprise or wonder (10)

Gave way (7)

Guard; watch (6)

Having a sturdy form or build (6)

Having or showing a clever or shrewd mind (6)

Hidden (9)

Imperfect; faulty (9)

Imprisonment (9)

In a manner feeling or showing hopelessness (12)

In a manner incapable of being disentangled (12)

In a manner not having anything to do with the matter at hand (12)

In a manner that is mysterious or obscure in meaning (11)

In a tired or worn-out manner (7)

Incapable of producing any result (6)

Insufficient to satisfy the need or demand (6)

Interwoven; wrapped around (6)

Listen secretly to a private conversation (9)

Made of materials from various sources (8)

Make an earnest request (5)

Making twisting or turning movements (8)

Mounted into and flush with the surface of an object (6)

Overhanging edges of a roof (5)

Period of partial darkness between day and night as the sun begins to set (4)

Put forth or use energetically (5)

Quieted; less active than usual (7)

Seriously; solemnly (7)

Side by side; beside each other in a line (7)

Spoken or read aloud to be written or recorded (8)

Strainer; a perforated pan used for draining liquids (8)

Stuck out; extended beyond (9)

Syringe or needle that injects medicine under the skin (10)

Terribly (10)

The outline of a figure, mass, land, etc. (7)

Upward slant (7)

Vague idea or notion (7)

Wandering about; going from place to place (6)

Mrs. Frisby and the Rats of NIMH Vocabulary Word Search 2

V	S	S	X	G	Q	R	E	S	F	H	H	S	K	T	Q	G	E	R	N
L	P	Y	G	A	H	J	L	H	E	R	M	I	T	R	D	N	A	O	Q
C	I	X	I	L	D	S	I	I	B	Z	F	Y	L	O	I	I	V	V	W
Z	N	G	B	E	V	I	T	N	I	A	L	P	D	Q	C	L	E	I	R
Y	Y	N	N	A	L	B	U	N	E	E	U	E	V	I	T	K	S	N	Q
Y	L	I	C	V	D	D	F	Y	V	X	T	X	M	Q	A	N	Y	G	Q
L	W	R	O	E	E	X	E	A	T	A	T	R	Z	S	T	I	P	G	P
T	P	E	R	S	B	D	R	D	T	S	E	R	E	M	E	R	G	E	D
N	A	T	R	D	R	G	H	I	X	D	R	U	I	T	D	N	C	X	L
A	R	L	I	R	I	C	S	S	O	I	E	O	U	C	D	R	T	E	X
V	T	I	D	O	S	E	F	P	R	M	D	T	J	T	A	U	B	R	W
E	I	F	O	P	H	H	Y	A	E	P	S	N	P	C	N	B	S	T	Y
L	T	S	R	L	H	H	R	T	C	A	I	O	S	E	D	M	L	K	K
E	I	A	H	E	N	C	O	C	E	S	N	C	I	P	D	Y	Z	Y	K
R	O	T	A	A	P	O	S	H	S	S	L	G	L	S	G	D	G	X	J
R	N	C	R	D	Y	N	R	E	S	E	A	G	O	O	H	P	L	G	D
I	S	H	R	G	K	F	U	D	E	P	I	H	S	R	W	T	L	E	H
M	P	E	O	W	Y	E	C	X	D	N	D	L	L	P	P	M	T	Z	R
D	Y	L	W	F	F	R	I	N	G	E	S	C	O	M	P	I	L	E	D

A very strong wind (4)

Agricultural implement with teeth or upright disks, for leveling and breaking up dirt clods (6)

Airtight pits or towers in which fodder is stored (5)

Any person living in seclusion (6)

At the outer edges or border (7)

Bits and pieces of rubbish; litter (6)

Came forth (7)

Climb by using both hands and legs for gripping (6)

Covered with thorns or prickles (5)

Discuss (6)

Dividers (10)

Expressing sorrow or melancholy (9)

Gave way (7)

Guard; watch (6)

Having a sturdy form or build (6)

Having or showing a clever or shrewd mind (6)

In a manner incapable of being disentangled (12)

In a manner not having anything to do with the matter at hand (12)

Incapable of producing any result (6)

Insufficient to satisfy the need or demand (6)

Interwoven; wrapped around (6)

Listen secretly to a private conversation (9)

Made of materials from various sources (8)

Make an earnest request (5)

Mounted into and flush with the surface of an object (6)

Outlook for the future (8)

Overhanging edges of a roof (5)

Passageway giving access to rooms, apartments, etc. (8)

Performed rapidly with little attention to detail (7)

Period of partial darkness between day and night as the sun begins to set (4)

Person who goes from place to place selling small articles (7)

Put forth or use energetically (5)

Sent off on a specific errand (10)

Seriously; solemnly (7)

Set back (8)

Situation offering no escape (7)

Slipping through slowly as if through an obstruction (9)

Small bag, sometimes with a shoulder strap (7)

Spoken or read aloud to be written or recorded (8)

Syringe or needle that injects medicine under the skin (10)

The outline of a figure, mass, land, etc. (7)

Vague idea or notion (7)

Wandering about; going from place to place (6)

Was reluctant or waited to act because of fear or indecision (9)

Waved or flapped about (9)

Mrs. Frisby and the Rats of NIMH Vocabulary Word Search 2 Answer Key

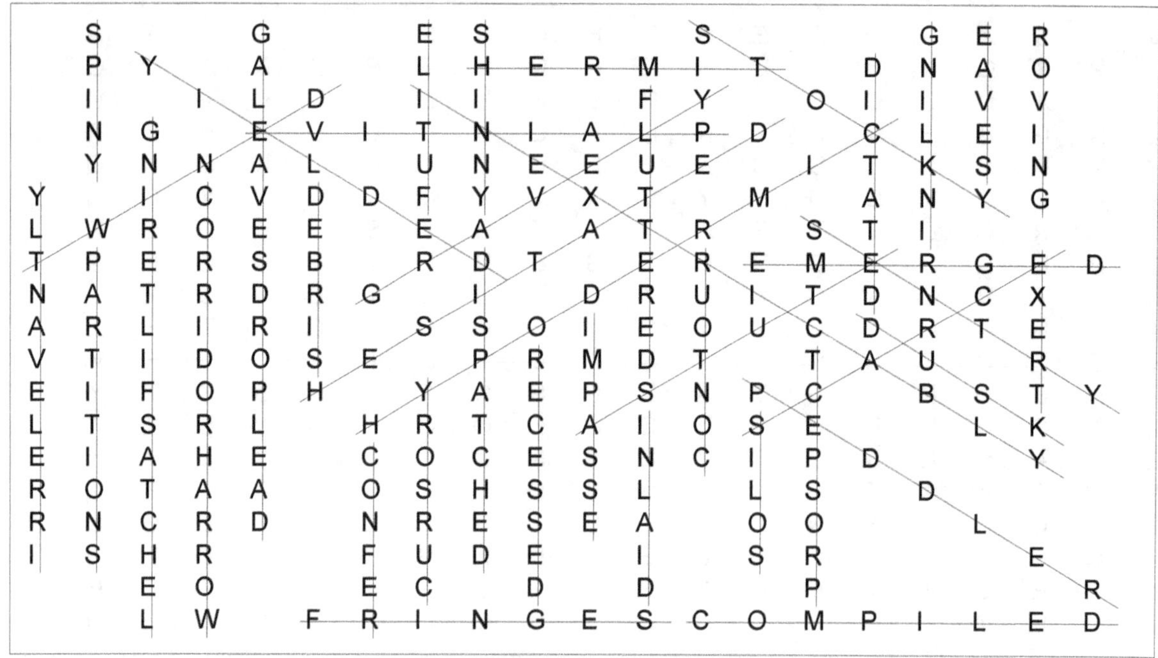

A very strong wind (4)
Agricultural implement with teeth or upright disks, for leveling and breaking up dirt clods (6)
Airtight pits or towers in which fodder is stored (5)
Any person living in seclusion (6)
At the outer edges or border (7)
Bits and pieces of rubbish; litter (6)
Came forth (7)
Climb by using both hands and legs for gripping (6)
Covered with thorns or prickles (5)
Discuss (6)
Dividers (10)
Expressing sorrow or melancholy (9)
Gave way (7)
Guard; watch (6)
Having a sturdy form or build (6)
Having or showing a clever or shrewd mind (6)
In a manner incapable of being disentangled (12)
In a manner not having anything to do with the matter at hand (12)
Incapable of producing any result (6)
Insufficient to satisfy the need or demand (6)
Interwoven; wrapped around (6)
Listen secretly to a private conversation (9)
Made of materials from various sources (8)
Make an earnest request (5)
Mounted into and flush with the surface of an object (6)
Outlook for the future (8)
Overhanging edges of a roof (5)
Passageway giving access to rooms, apartments, etc. (8)
Performed rapidly with little attention to detail (7)
Period of partial darkness between day and night as the sun begins to set (4)
Person who goes from place to place selling small articles (7)
Put forth or use energetically (5)
Sent off on a specific errand (10)
Seriously; solemnly (7)
Set back (8)
Situation offering no escape (7)
Slipping through slowly as if through an obstruction (9)
Small bag, sometimes with a shoulder strap (7)
Spoken or read aloud to be written or recorded (8)
Syringe or needle that injects medicine under the skin (10)
The outline of a figure, mass, land, etc. (7)
Vague idea or notion (7)
Wandering about; going from place to place (6)
Was reluctant or waited to act because of fear or indecision (9)
Waved or flapped about (9)

```
H  E  S  I  T  A  T  E  D  P  L  A  I  N  T  I  V  E  T  Y
A  L  S  C  N  R  S  E  V  A  E  C  D  Y  R  Y  M  N  D  S
R  E  S  O  H  C  D  L  C  D  D  E  T  M  R  E  A  E  I  T
R  G  P  R  C  L  U  I  E  E  D  I  F  E  R  C  B  P  A  G
O  A  I  D  E  R  N  R  T  U  V  U  D  G  A  R  M  I  L  T
W  N  N  I  H  Y  U  A  R  I  T  N  E  V  I  V  C  D  N  F
C  T  Y  A  C  T  T  T  T  I  A  D  S  S  C  E  C  E  I  G
O  L  Y  L  N  C  O  P  L  L  N  F  P  I  O  N  D  M  N  F
M  Y  M  E  I  R  A  E  O  S  C  G  A  L  R  T  E  I  D  R
P  L  V  D  P  C  J  C  T  Y  O  C  I  O  R  I  F  C  I  H
I  T  W  T  R  K  T  P  D  L  N  U  R  S  I  L  E  L  G  R
L  N  L  R  O  O  G  W  N  E  F  R  I  X  D  A  C  B  N  N
E  A  J  S  I  I  N  F  L  V  E  S  N  L  O  T  T  X  A  V
D  V  Q  H  N  T  L  I  B  A  R  O  G  C  R  I  I  L  N  C
B  E  K  I  G  G  H  I  N  R  Y  R  L  K  O  O  V  D  T  H
X  L  U  N  E  R  R  I  N  G  L  Y  Y  R  T  N  E  S  L  Z
N  E  R  N  V  D  W  B  N  G  K  K  E  V  W  H  T  E  Y  X
F  R  O  Y  E  G  P  I  R  G  C  E  C  L  C  H  H  O  V  J
B  R  V  N  W  D  L  R  S  O  T  I  R  T  X  C  R  I  U  J
Y  I  I  T  J  K  E  Y  T  U  M  V  A  N  T  A  G  E  H  R
Z  W  N  N  N  B  A  S  T  P  B  P  C  A  C  O  A  X  E  V
T  B  G  I  G  K  D  S  A  J  S  D  S  D  R  W  L  E  R  T
C  S  A  B  R  E  A  S  T  I  D  K  U  O  Y  V  E  R  M  J
K  V  T  N  E  C  S  E  D  P  K  S  U  E  D  F  G  T  I  S
P  E  D  D  L  E  R  H  Y  R  K  S  R  R  D  L  Q  L  T  Y
```

ABREAST	DEFECTIVE	FRINGES	IRRELEVANTLY	STOCKY
ASTUTE	DESCENT	FUTILE	PEDDLER	SUBDUED
CAPTIVITY	DESPAIRINGLY	GALE	PLAINTIVE	TOILING
COLANDER	DICTATED	GRAVELY	PLEAD	TWINED
COMPILED	DISPATCHED	HARROW	PROTRUDED	UNERRINGLY
CONFER	DRONING	HERMIT	ROVING	VACANT
CONTOUR	DUSK	HESITATED	SATCHEL	VANTAGE
CORDIAL	EAVES	IMPASSE	SCARCE	VENTILATION
CORRIDOR	ELEGANTLY	INCURRING	SENTRY	VENTURED
CURSORY	EMERGED	INDIGNANTLY	SHINNY	VIGOROUS
CYNICAL	EPIDEMIC	INKLING	SILOS	WRITHING
DEBRIS	EXERT	INLAID	SPINY	YIELDED

Mrs. Frisby and the Rats of NIMH Vocabulary Word Search 3 Answer Key

```
H E S I T A T E D P L A I N T I V E T
A L   C N   S E V A E   D Y       M N D
R E S O   C D   C D D E T   R E A E   I
R G P R   L U I   E E D I F E R C B P A
O A I D E   N R T U V U D G A R   I   L
W N N I   Y U A R I T N E V I V   D   N
C T Y A C T T T I A D S S C E   E   I
O L L N C O P L L N P I O N D M N
M Y E I R A E O   C G A L R T E I D
P L V D P C   C   Y O C I O R I F C I
I T W T R     O   N C R I S I L     G
L N   R O O N     C U I D   A   C   N
E A   S I   N     V F S I   O   T   A
D V   H T L I   A R O G C R I     N
  E   H I N R R O L Y   D T
L U N E R R I N G L Y Y R T N E S L
E R N   D   N G   K E       H   E Y
F R O Y E P I G C E   C   C H O I U
R V N   L S O T I R T   C I E H
I   K E T U M V A N T A G E   R
W N N N A S T P B P C A   O A X H R
T G I G D S A S D S D R   L E E M
A B R E A S T I     U O   E R M
T N E C S E D     S U E     T I
P E D D L E R     K S   D       T
```

ABREAST	DEFECTIVE	FRINGES	IRRELEVANTLY	STOCKY
ASTUTE	DESCENT	FUTILE	PEDDLER	SUBDUED
CAPTIVITY	DESPAIRINGLY	GALE	PLAINTIVE	TOILING
COLANDER	DICTATED	GRAVELY	PLEAD	TWINED
COMPILED	DISPATCHED	HARROW	PROTRUDED	UNERRINGLY
CONFER	DRONING	HERMIT	ROVING	VACANT
CONTOUR	DUSK	HESITATED	SATCHEL	VANTAGE
CORDIAL	EAVES	IMPASSE	SCARCE	VENTILATION
CORRIDOR	ELEGANTLY	INCURRING	SENTRY	VENTURED
CURSORY	EMERGED	INDIGNANTLY	SHINNY	VIGOROUS
CYNICAL	EPIDEMIC	INKLING	SILOS	WRITHING
DEBRIS	EXERT	INLAID	SPINY	YIELDED

```
H E R M I T V E N T I L A T I O N C P X
R W F R I N G E S N D W C M G D R A O F
D R O N I N G R E G X O Z C F E E P R T
S I R B E D X X A Z N C K M O G L T D X
S T O C K Y O E A V E S O A L R D I S K
V H S V C R P M E N E J Q N G E D V E P
A I G T A N V R D A E L P I C M E I V Q
R N S B R N G E O X A P Y P O E P T A S
T G L D P E T M N T B P B U M Y A Y E L
I E A E D N N A Y T R X N L P L P L H K
F I L U X L E K G N U U Y A I I Y F E Q
I N G D T Z T S S E P R D T L R R U Y D
C K A B L H N U Y C T D E E E A T T Q W
I L L U S I O N I N L A I D D E N I W T
A I E S N R C R W N Y U E C N W E L D Z
L N T R O H S Q I S D T T I T B S E Y L
V G O G J Q I C E T A I L T W A T Y I H
S H I N N Y D T A T A C G R E A T Z E L
C V L M P C I Y I R N T J N V R T E L R
O K I E P P D G R I C V I I A N E S D P
N M N X S A A S T U T E T V A N O D E H
F K G E D M S P I N Y L X C E L T W D N
E M R R Y Z G S P R U F A F I L W L R C
R P M T D U S K E C Z V D S P D Y L Y R
```

ABRUPTLY	DICTATED	IMPASSE	SILOS
AGITATED	DISCONTENT	INCLINE	SPINY
ARTIFICIAL	DRONING	INDIGNANTLY	STOCKY
ASTUTE	DUSK	INEXORABLE	SUBDUED
AUTHORITATIVELY	EAVES	INKLING	TOILING
CAPTIVITY	EAVESDROP	INLAID	TWINED
CLUTTERED	EMERGED	MANIPULATED	VACANT
COMPILED	EXERT	PEDDLER	VANTAGE
CONCEALED	FRINGES	PLEAD	VENTILATION
CONFER	FUTILE	PROTRUDED	VENTURED
CONVERGED	GALE	RESPITE	VIGOROUS
CORDIAL	GRAVELY	SCARCE	WEARILY
CULTIVATED	HERMIT	SENTRY	WRITHING
DEBRIS	ILLUSION	SHINNY	YIELDED

Mrs. Frisby and the Rats of NIMH Vocabulary Word Search 4 Answer Key

ABRUPTLY

AGITATED

ARTIFICIAL

ASTUTE

AUTHORITATIVELY

CAPTIVITY

CLUTTERED

COMPILED

CONCEALED

CONFER

CONVERGED

CORDIAL

CULTIVATED

DEBRIS

DICTATED

DISCONTENT

DRONING

DUSK

EAVES

EAVESDROP

EMERGED

EXERT

FRINGES

FUTILE

GALE

GRAVELY

HERMIT

ILLUSION

IMPASSE

INCLINE

INDIGNANTLY

INEXORABLE

INKLING

INLAID

MANIPULATED

PEDDLER

PLEAD

PROTRUDED

RESPITE

SCARCE

SENTRY

SHINNY

SILOS

SPINY

STOCKY

SUBDUED

TOILING

TWINED

VACANT

VANTAGE

VENTILATION

VENTURED

VIGOROUS

WEARILY

WRITHING

YIELDED

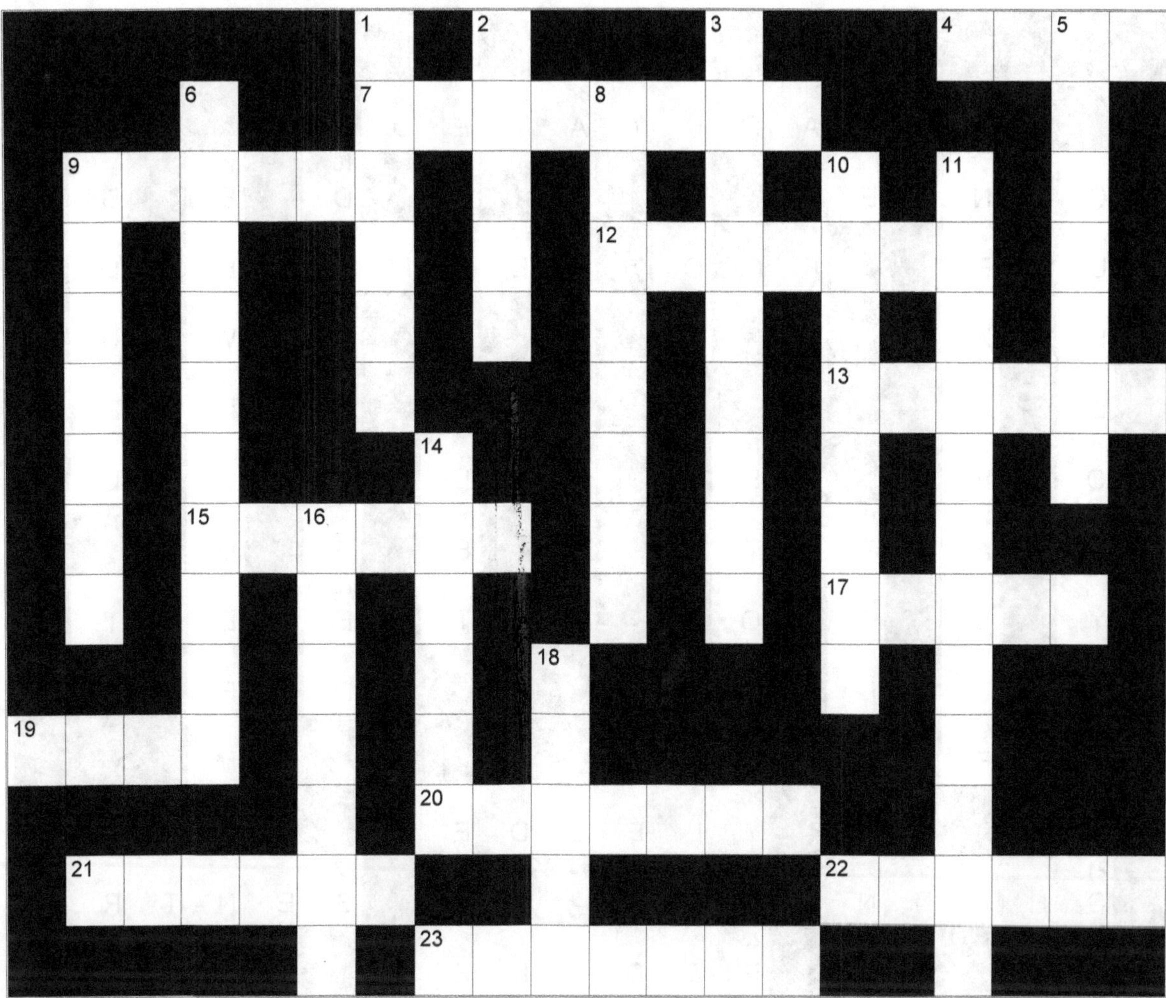

Mrs. Frisby and the Rats of NIMH Vocabulary Crossword 1

Across

4. Period of partial darkness between day and night as the sun begins to set
7. Troubled or nervous
9. Discuss
12. A break
13. Interwoven; wrapped around
15. Having or showing a clever or shrewd mind
17. Put forth or use energetically
19. A very strong wind
20. Gave way
21. Climb by using both hands and legs for gripping
22. Guard; watch
23. Person who goes from place to place selling small articles

Down

1. Agricultural implement with teeth or upright disks, for leveling and breaking up dirt clods
2. Airtight pits or towers in which fodder is stored
3. Person who sees everything in a negative or the worst possible way
5. Quieted; less active than usual
6. Such that cannot be moved or influenced by persuasion
8. Suddenly or unexpectedly
9. Performed rapidly with little attention to detail
10. Spoken or read aloud to be written or recorded
11. The condition of being completely puzzled
14. Having a sturdy form or build
16. Working with exhausting labor or effort
18. Make an earnest request

Mrs. Frisby and the Rats of NIMH Vocabulary Crossword 1 Answer Key

Across

4. Period of partial darkness between day and night as the sun begins to set
7. Troubled or nervous
9. Discuss
12. A break
13. Interwoven; wrapped around
15. Having or showing a clever or shrewd mind
17. Put forth or use energetically
19. A very strong wind
20. Gave way
21. Climb by using both hands and legs for gripping
22. Guard; watch
23. Person who goes from place to place selling small articles

Down

1. Agricultural implement with teeth or upright disks, for leveling and breaking up dirt clods
2. Airtight pits or towers in which fodder is stored
3. Person who sees everything in a negative or the worst possible way
5. Quieted; less active than usual
6. Such that cannot be moved or influenced by persuasion
8. Suddenly or unexpectedly
9. Performed rapidly with little attention to detail
10. Spoken or read aloud to be written or recorded
11. The condition of being completely puzzled
14. Having a sturdy form or build
16. Working with exhausting labor or effort
18. Make an earnest request

Mrs. Frisby and the Rats of NIMH Vocabulary Crossword 2

Across

1. Seriously; solemnly
7. Mounted into and flush with the surface of an object
9. Suddenly or unexpectedly
13. Interwoven; wrapped around
14. Dividers
16. Bits and pieces of rubbish; litter
18. Overhanging edges of a roof
20. Period of partial darkness between day and night as the sun begins to set
21. Having a sturdy form or build
22. Person who sees everything in a negative or the worst possible way
23. Working with exhausting labor or effort

Down

1. A very strong wind
2. Put forth or use energetically
3. Gave way
4. Waved or flapped about
5. Worked, operated, or treated with the hands
6. Stuck out; extended beyond
8. Furnace or apparatus for burning materials
10. Expressing sorrow or melancholy
11. Position that provides a clear, broad view
12. Set back
15. Upward slant
17. The moving from a higher to a lower place
19. Having or showing a clever or shrewd mind

Mrs. Frisby and the Rats of NIMH Vocabulary Crossword 2 Answer Key

Across
1. Seriously; solemnly
7. Mounted into and flush with the surface of an object
9. Suddenly or unexpectedly
13. Interwoven; wrapped around
14. Dividers
16. Bits and pieces of rubbish; litter
18. Overhanging edges of a roof
20. Period of partial darkness between day and night as the sun begins to set
21. Having a sturdy form or build
22. Person who sees everything in a negative or the worst possible way
23. Working with exhausting labor or effort

Down
1. A very strong wind
2. Put forth or use energetically
3. Gave way
4. Waved or flapped about
5. Worked, operated, or treated with the hands
6. Stuck out; extended beyond
8. Furnace or apparatus for burning materials
10. Expressing sorrow or melancholy
11. Position that provides a clear, broad view
12. Set back
15. Upward slant
17. The moving from a higher to a lower place
19. Having or showing a clever or shrewd mind

Mrs. Frisby and the Rats of NIMH Vocabulary Crossword 3

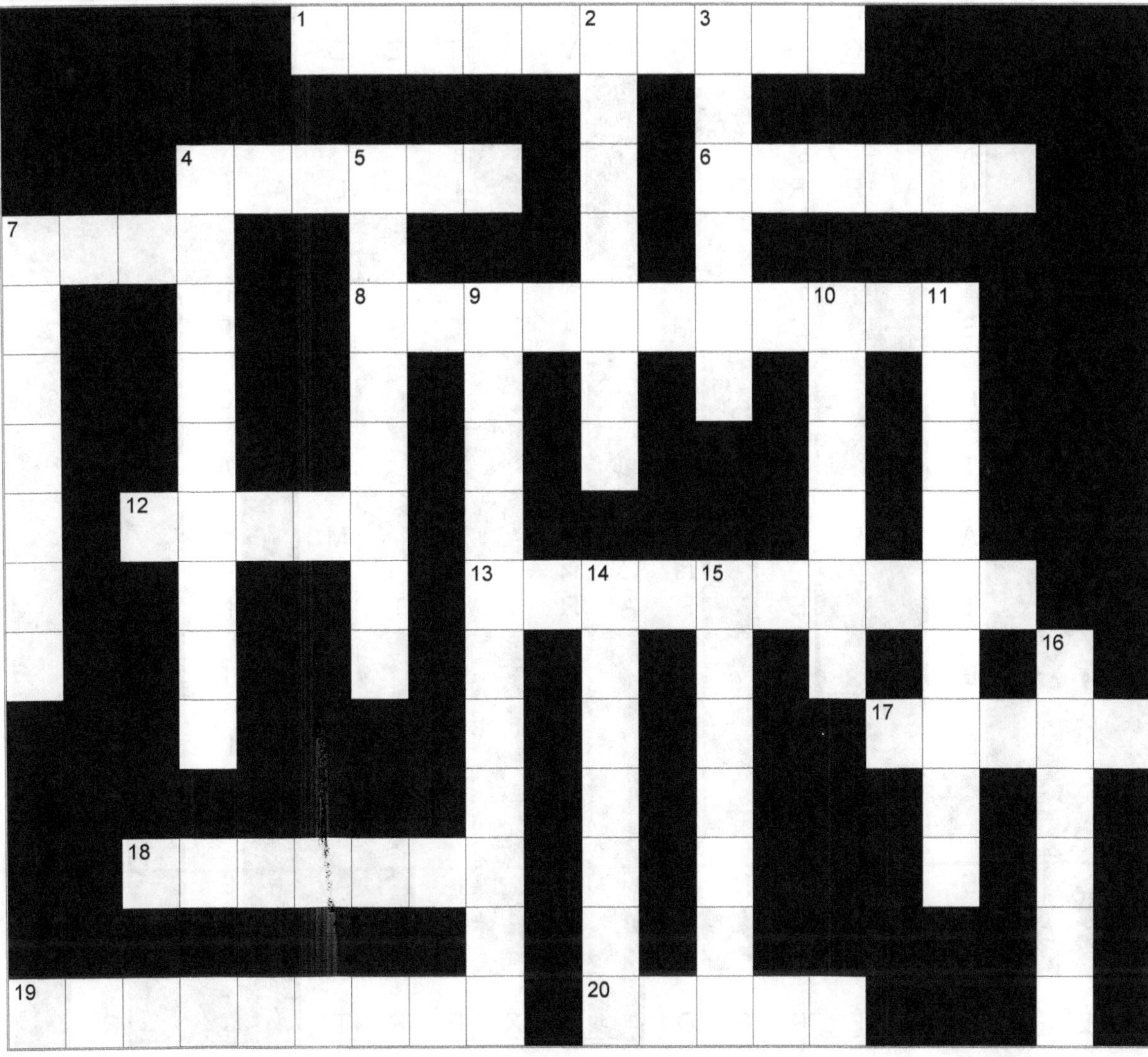

Across

1. Prepared for growing crops; tended; nurtured
4. Agricultural implement with teeth or upright disks, for leveling and breaking up dirt clods
6. Mounted into and flush with the surface of an object
7. A very strong wind
8. Friendship; companionship
12. Overhanging edges of a roof
13. Dividers
17. Airtight pits or towers in which fodder is stored
18. The moving from a higher to a lower place
19. Waved or flapped about
20. Put forth or use energetically

Down

2. Position that provides a clear, broad view
3. Interwoven; wrapped around
4. Was reluctant or waited to act because of fear or indecision
5. Set back
7. Seriously; solemnly
9. Worked, operated, or treated with the hands
10. Any person living in seclusion
11. Expressing sorrow or melancholy
14. A break
15. Upward slant
16. Discuss

Mrs. Frisby and the Rats of NIMH Vocabulary Crossword 3 Answer Key

Across

1. Prepared for growing crops; tended; nurtured
4. Agricultural implement with teeth or upright disks, for leveling and breaking up dirt clods
6. Mounted into and flush with the surface of an object
7. A very strong wind
8. Friendship; companionship
12. Overhanging edges of a roof
13. Dividers
17. Airtight pits or towers in which fodder is stored
18. The moving from a higher to a lower place
19. Waved or flapped about
20. Put forth or use energetically

Down

2. Position that provides a clear, broad view
3. Interwoven; wrapped around
4. Was reluctant or waited to act because of fear or indecision
5. Set back
7. Seriously; solemnly
9. Worked, operated, or treated with the hands
10. Any person living in seclusion
11. Expressing sorrow or melancholy
14. A break
15. Upward slant
16. Discuss

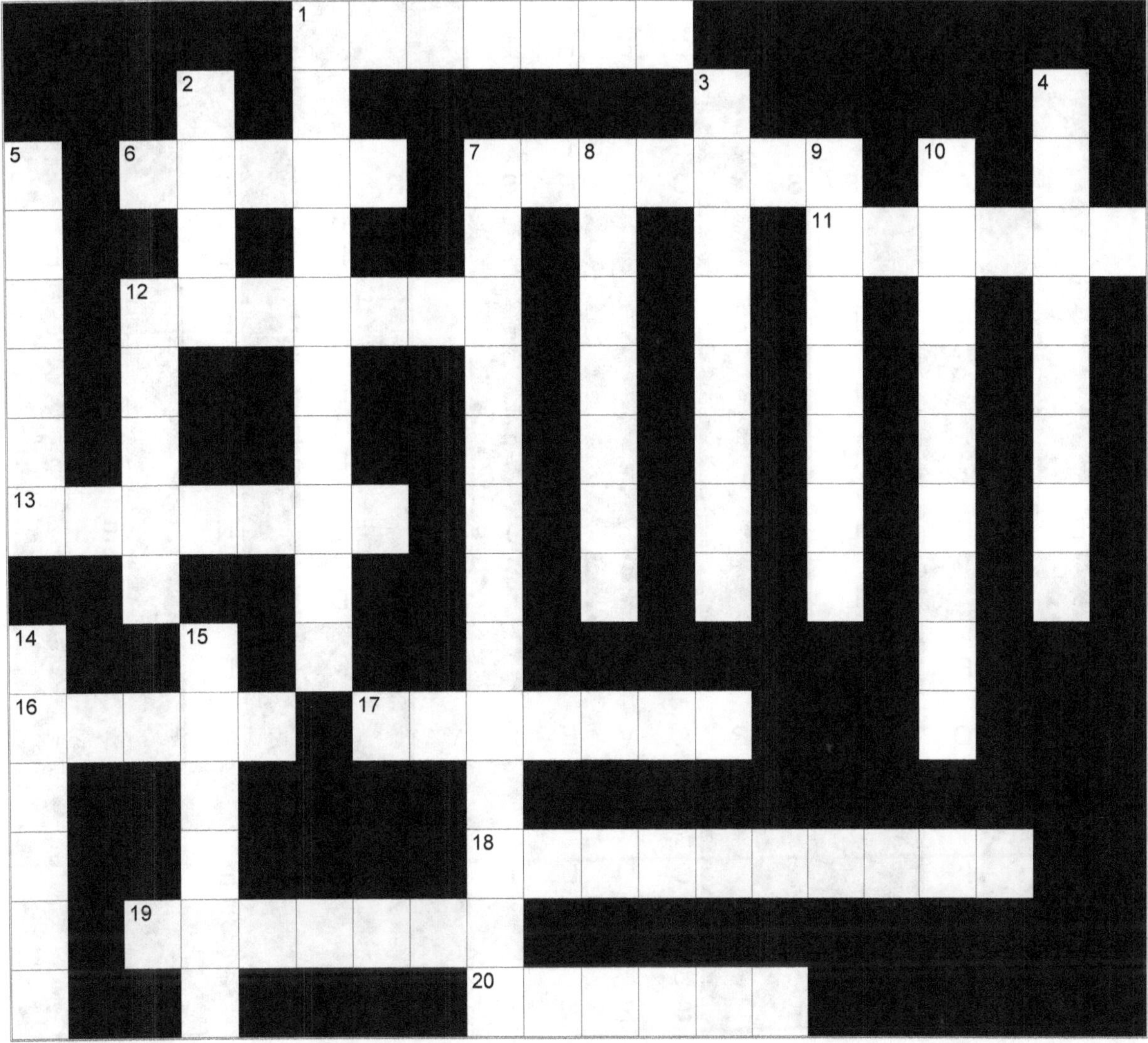

Across

1. The moving from a higher to a lower place
6. Overhanging edges of a roof
7. Performed rapidly with little attention to detail
11. Mounted into and flush with the surface of an object
12. Person who goes from place to place selling small articles
13. In a tired or worn-out manner
16. Airtight pits or towers in which fodder is stored
17. Seriously; solemnly
18. Prepared for growing crops; tended; nurtured
19. Upward slant
20. Guard; watch

Down

1. Terribly
2. A very strong wind
3. Strainer; a perforated pan used for draining liquids
4. Troubled or nervous
5. Agricultural implement with teeth or upright disks, for leveling and breaking up dirt clods
7. Conditions surrounding an event
8. A break
9. Gave way
10. In a splendid or luxurious style or design
12. Make an earnest request
14. Having or showing a clever or shrewd mind
15. Wandering about; going from place to place

Mrs. Frisby and the Rats of NIMH Vocabulary Crossword 4 Answer Key

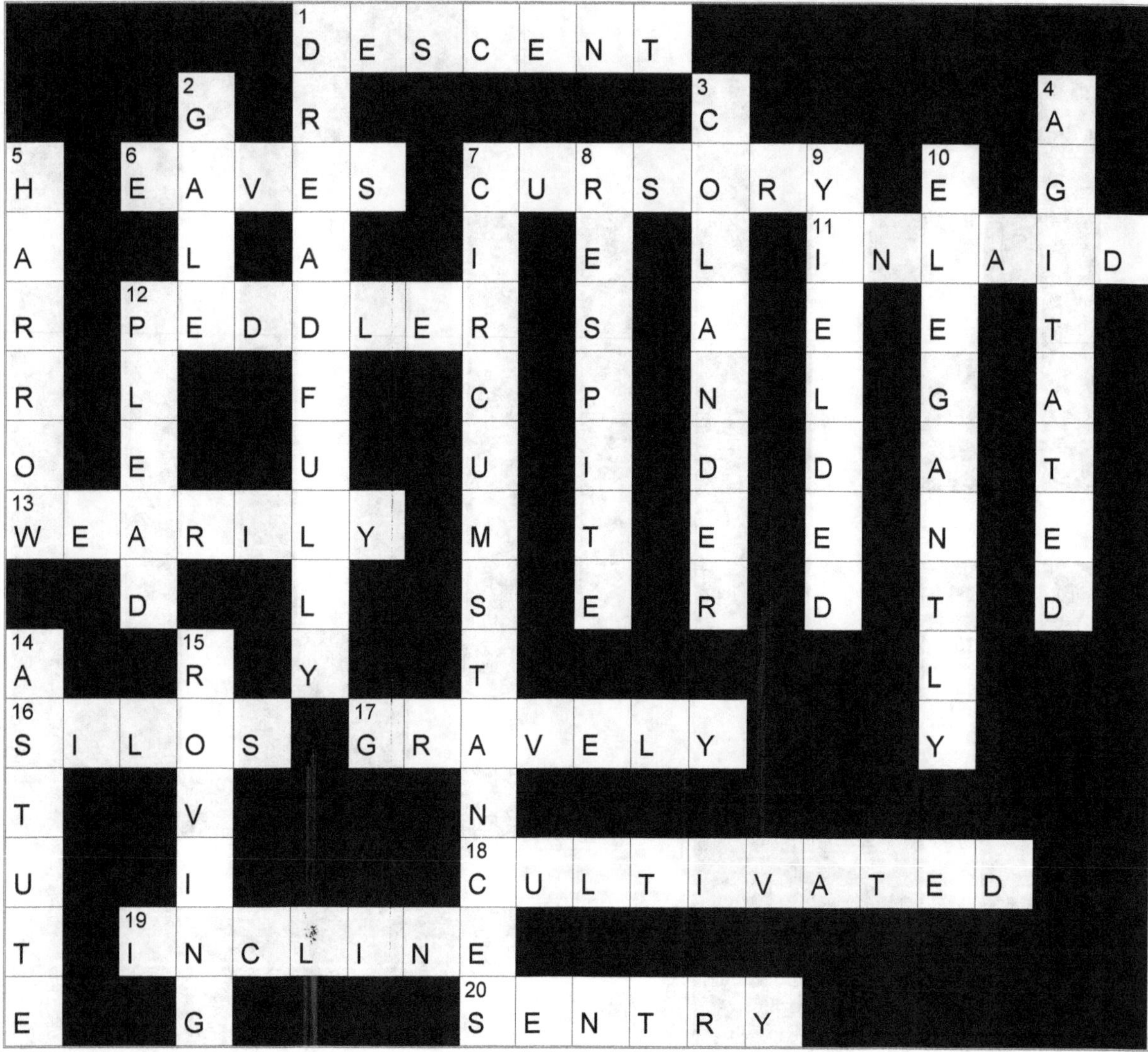

Across
1. The moving from a higher to a lower place
6. Overhanging edges of a roof
7. Performed rapidly with little attention to detail
11. Mounted into and flush with the surface of an object
12. Person who goes from place to place selling small articles
13. In a tired or worn-out manner
16. Airtight pits or towers in which fodder is stored
17. Seriously; solemnly
18. Prepared for growing crops; tended; nurtured
19. Upward slant
20. Guard; watch
.

Down
1. Terribly
2. A very strong wind
3. Strainer; a perforated pan used for draining liquids
4. Troubled or nervous
5. Agricultural implement with teeth or upright disks, for leveling and breaking up dirt clods
7. Conditions surrounding an event
8. A break
9. Gave way
10. In a splendid or luxurious style or design
12. Make an earnest request
14. Having or showing a clever or shrewd mind
15. Wandering about; going from place to place

Mrs. Frisby and the Rats of NIMH Vocabulary Juggle Letters 1

1. IORAPSTIRNPE   = 1. _______________________
                             Sweat

2. OPVDEAERS   = 2. _______________________
                             Listen secretly to a private conversation

3. ESCATHL   = 3. _______________________
                             Small bag, sometimes with a shoulder strap

4. EANOTSNOTNIRC   = 4. _______________________
                             Feeling of helplessness due to great fear or shock

5. TYRBLPAU   = 5. _______________________
                             Suddenly or unexpectedly

6. RITWHING   = 6. _______________________
                             Making twisting or turning movements

7. CRDESEES   = 7. _______________________
                             Set back

8. EMSSIPA   = 8. _______________________
                             Situation offering no escape

9. EEIRTPS   = 9. _______________________
                             A break

10. MTEHRI   =10. _______________________
                             Any person living in seclusion

11. ANEBLEORIX   =11. _______________________
                             Such that cannot be moved or influenced by persuasion

12. TLEAGYLEN   =12. _______________________
                             In a splendid or luxurious style or design

13. DNOHDIMAES   =13. _______________________
                             Mildly scolded; spoken to in disapproval

14. NGINROD   =14. _______________________
                             Making a continuous, low, monotonous sound

Mrs. Frisby and the Rats of NIMH Vocabulary Juggle Letters 1 Answer Key

1. IORAPSTIRNPE   = 1. PERSPIRATION
                                   Sweat

2. OPVDEAERS   = 2. EAVESDROP
                                   Listen secretly to a private conversation

3. ESCATHL   = 3. SATCHEL
                                   Small bag, sometimes with a shoulder strap

4. EANOTSNOTNIRC   = 4. CONSTERNATION
                                   Feeling of helplessness due to great fear or shock

5. TYRBLPAU   = 5. ABRUPTLY
                                   Suddenly or unexpectedly

6. RITWHING   = 6. WRITHING
                                   Making twisting or turning movements

7. CRDESEES   = 7. RECESSED
                                   Set back

8. EMSSIPA   = 8. IMPASSE
                                   Situation offering no escape

9. EEIRTPS   = 9. RESPITE
                                   A break

10. MTEHRI   =10. HERMIT
                                   Any person living in seclusion

11. ANEBLEORIX   =11. INEXORABLE
                                   Such that cannot be moved or influenced by persuasion

12. TLEAGYLEN   =12. ELEGANTLY
                                   In a splendid or luxurious style or design

13. DNOHDIMAES   =13. ADMONISHED
                                   Mildly scolded; spoken to in disapproval

14. NGINROD   =14. DRONING
                                   Making a continuous, low, monotonous sound

Mrs. Frisby and the Rats of NIMH Vocabulary Juggle Letters 2

1. BEEARDETILLY   = 1. _______________________

Intentionally; on purpose; with forethought

2. CSACRE   = 2. _______________________

Insufficient to satisfy the need or demand

3. GIIRRNUCN   = 3. _______________________

Bringing upon oneself

4. IYTNDNAIGNL   = 4. _______________________

In a manner expressing great anger or scorn

5. LEITFU   = 5. _______________________

Incapable of producing any result

6. MEBRLGTIN   = 6. _______________________

Shaking involuntarily with quick, short movements as from
fear, excitement, or cold

7. AESTHLC   = 7. _______________________

Small bag, sometimes with a shoulder strap

8. ISAPTINTOR   = 8. _______________________

Dividers

9. INOLNTVIEAT   = 9. _______________________

System that circulates air

10. DMPCEOIL   =10. _______________________

Made of materials from various sources

11. ITPNESAROPIR   =11. _______________________

Sweat

12. DCCAOLNEE   =12. _______________________

Hidden

13. DEPREASVO   =13. _______________________

Listen secretly to a private conversation

14. DRAODEJNU   =14. _______________________

Suspended (a meeting) until a later time or another place

Mrs. Frisby and the Rats of NIMH Vocabulary Juggle Letters 2 Answer Key

1. BEEARDETILLY = 1. DELIBERATELY
   Intentionally; on purpose; with forethought

2. CSACRE = 2. SCARCE
   Insufficient to satisfy the need or demand

3. GIIRRNUCN = 3. INCURRING
   Bringing upon oneself

4. IYTNDNAIGNL = 4. INDIGNANTLY
   In a manner expressing great anger or scorn

5. LEITFU = 5. FUTILE
   Incapable of producing any result

6. MEBRLGTIN = 6. TREMBLING
   Shaking involuntarily with quick, short movements as from
   fear, excitement, or cold

7. AESTHLC = 7. SATCHEL
   Small bag, sometimes with a shoulder strap

8. ISAPTINTOR = 8. PARTITIONS
   Dividers

9. INOLNTVIEAT = 9. VENTILATION
   System that circulates air

10. DMPCEOIL =10. COMPILED
   Made of materials from various sources

11. ITPNESAROPIR =11. PERSPIRATION
   Sweat

12. DCCAOLNEE =12. CONCEALED
   Hidden

13. DEPREASVO =13. EAVESDROP
   Listen secretly to a private conversation

14. DRAODEJNU =14. ADJOURNED
   Suspended (a meeting) until a later time or another place

1. LCUTREEDT   = 1. ________________________
Containing too many things, often unorganized

2. PHCEDTASID   = 2. ________________________
Sent off on a specific errand

3. IVETCUTLDA   = 3. ________________________
Prepared for growing crops; tended; nurtured

4. LTIVOANENIT   = 4. ________________________
System that circulates air

5. CVNTAA   = 5. ________________________
Empty

6. ULIOLNSI   = 6. ________________________
Something that deceives by producing a false impression of reality

7. PTIDXONEEI   = 7. ________________________
Journey or voyage made for a specific purpose

8. RRGIUYENNL   = 8. ________________________
Without mistakes

9. RCROODIR   = 9. ________________________
Passageway giving access to rooms, apartments, etc.

10. PYCHEOIRDM   =10. ________________________
Syringe or needle that injects medicine under the skin

11. ETHSALC   =11. ________________________
Small bag, sometimes with a shoulder strap

12. AOIINRTPTS   =12. ________________________
Dividers

13. RSEIGFN   =13. ________________________
At the outer edges or border

14. YRDNEIGSAPLI   =14. ________________________
In a manner feeling or showing hopelessness

Mrs. Frisby and the Rats of NIMH Vocabulary Juggle Letters 3 Answer Key

1. LCUTREEDT   = 1. CLUTTERED
Containing too many things, often unorganized

2. PHCEDTASID   = 2. DISPATCHED
Sent off on a specific errand

3. IVETCUTLDA   = 3. CULTIVATED
Prepared for growing crops; tended; nurtured

4. LTIVOANENIT   = 4. VENTILATION
System that circulates air

5. CVNTAA   = 5. VACANT
Empty

6. ULIOLNSI   = 6. ILLUSION
Something that deceives by producing a false impression of reality

7. PTIDXONEEI   = 7. EXPEDITION
Journey or voyage made for a specific purpose

8. RRGIUYENNL   = 8. UNERRINGLY
Without mistakes

9. RCROODIR   = 9. CORRIDOR
Passageway giving access to rooms, apartments, etc.

10. PYCHEOIRDM   =10. HYPODERMIC
Syringe or needle that injects medicine under the skin

11. ETHSALC   =11. SATCHEL
Small bag, sometimes with a shoulder strap

12. AOIINRTPTS   =12. PARTITIONS
Dividers

13. RSEIGFN   =13. FRINGES
At the outer edges or border

14. YRDNEIGSAPLI   =14. DESPAIRINGLY
In a manner feeling or showing hopelessness

1. ISPNY   = 1. ___________________________
                         Covered with thorns or prickles

2. GSOUOIRV   = 2. ___________________________
                         Strong; active; robust

3. TLRAHEIITYUATOV   = 3. ___________________________
                         In a commanding way

4. TAEITHDES   = 4. ___________________________
                         Was reluctant or waited to act because of fear or indecision

5. HEODCARMSIP   = 5. ___________________________
                         Friendship; companionship

6. SIMOEADHND   = 6. ___________________________
                         Mildly scolded; spoken to in disapproval

7. TXEER   = 7. ___________________________
                         Put forth or use energetically

8. RCNUOOT   = 8. ___________________________
                         The outline of a figure, mass, land, etc.

9. ANETRLLIVEYR   = 9. ___________________________
                         In a manner not having anything to do with the matter at hand

10. RSYCUOR   =10. ___________________________
                         Performed rapidly with little attention to detail

11. BLXREACIITNY   =11. ___________________________
                         In a manner incapable of being disentangled

12. IRRTNOIPESAP   =12. ___________________________
                         Sweat

13. EONTCTRSANION   =13. ___________________________
                         Feeling of helplessness due to great fear or shock

14. STPTAORNII   =14. ___________________________
                         Dividers

Mrs. Frisby and the Rats of NIMH Vocabulary Juggle Letters 4 Answer Key

1. ISPNY = 1. SPINY
Covered with thorns or prickles

2. GSOUOIRV = 2. VIGOROUS
Strong; active; robust

3. TLRAHEIITYUATOV = 3. AUTHORITATIVELY
In a commanding way

4. TAEITHDES = 4. HESITATED
Was reluctant or waited to act because of fear or indecision

5. HEODCARMSIP = 5. COMRADESHIP
Friendship; companionship

6. SIMOEADHND = 6. ADMONISHED
Mildly scolded; spoken to in disapproval

7. TXEER = 7. EXERT
Put forth or use energetically

8. RCNUOOT = 8. CONTOUR
The outline of a figure, mass, land, etc.

9. ANETRLLIVEYR = 9. IRRELEVANTLY
In a manner not having anything to do with the matter at hand

10. RSYCUOR =10. CURSORY
Performed rapidly with little attention to detail

11. BLXREACIITNY =11. INEXTRICABLY
In a manner incapable of being disentangled

12. IRRTNOIPESAP =12. PERSPIRATION
Sweat

13. EONTCTRSANION =13. CONSTERNATION
Feeling of helplessness due to great fear or shock

14. STPTAORNII =14. PARTITIONS
Dividers

ABREAST	Side by side; beside each other in a line
ABRUPTLY	Suddenly or unexpectedly
ADJOURNED	Suspended (a meeting) until a later time or another place
ADMONISHED	Mildly scolded; spoken to in disapproval
AGITATED	Troubled or nervous
ARTIFICIAL	Made by human work or art, not by nature

ASTONISHED	Filled with sudden, overpowering surprise or wonder
ASTUTE	Having or showing a clever or shrewd mind
AUTHORITATIVELY	In a commanding way
BEWILDERMENT	The condition of being completely puzzled
CAPTIVITY	Imprisonment
CIRCUMSTANCES	Conditions surrounding an event

CLUTTERED	Containing too many things, often unorganized
COLANDER	Strainer; a perforated pan used for draining liquids
COMPILED	Made of materials from various sources
COMRADESHIP	Friendship; companionship
CONCEALED	Hidden
CONFER	Discuss

CONSTERNATION	Feeling of helplessness due to great fear or shock
CONTOUR	The outline of a figure, mass, land, etc.
CONVERGED	Came together to meet at a point or in a line
CORDIAL	Courteous; gracious; friendly
CORRIDOR	Passageway giving access to rooms, apartments, etc.
CRYPTICALLY	In a manner that is mysterious or obscure in meaning

CULTIVATED	Prepared for growing crops; tended; nurtured
CURSORY	Performed rapidly with little attention to detail
CYNICAL	Believing that people are only motivated by selfishness
DEBRIS	Bits and pieces of rubbish; litter
DEFECTIVE	Imperfect; faulty
DELIBERATELY	Intentionally; on purpose; with forethought

DESCENT	The moving from a higher to a lower place
DESPAIRINGLY	In a manner feeling or showing hopelessness
DICTATED	Spoken or read aloud to be written or recorded
DISCONTENT	Dissatisfaction; a restless desire for something more
DISPATCHED	Sent off on a specific errand
DREADFULLY	Terribly

DRONING	Making a continuous, low, monotonous sound
DUSK	Period of partial darkness between day and night as the sun begins to set
EAVES	Overhanging edges of a roof
EAVESDROP	Listen secretly to a private conversation
ELEGANTLY	In a splendid or luxurious style or design
EMERGED	Came forth

EPIDEMIC	Prevalent and spreading rapidly among many individuals
EXERT	Put forth or use energetically
EXPEDITION	Journey or voyage made for a specific purpose
FILTERING	Slipping through slowly as if through an obstruction
FLUTTERED	Waved or flapped about
FRINGES	At the outer edges or border

FUTILE	Incapable of producing any result
GALE	A very strong wind
GRAVELY	Seriously; solemnly
HARROW	Agricultural implement with teeth or upright disks, for leveling and breaking up dirt clods
HERMIT	Any person living in seclusion
HESITATED	Was reluctant or waited to act because of fear or indecision

HYPODERMIC	Syringe or needle that injects medicine under the skin
ILLUSION	Something that deceives by producing a false impression of reality
IMPASSE	Situation offering no escape
INCINERATOR	Furnace or apparatus for burning materials
INCLINE	Upward slant
INCURRING	Bringing upon oneself

INDIGNANTLY	In a manner expressing great anger or scorn
INEXORABLE	Such that cannot be moved or influenced by persuasion
INEXTRICABLY	In a manner incapable of being disentangled
INKLING	Vague idea or notion
INLAID	Mounted into and flush with the surface of an object
IRRELEVANTLY	In a manner not having anything to do with the matter at hand

MANIPULATED	Worked, operated, or treated with the hands
PARTITIONS	Dividers
PEDDLER	Person who goes from place to place selling small articles
PERSPIRATION	Sweat
PESSIMIST	Person who sees everything in a negative or the worst possible way
PLAINTIVE	Expressing sorrow or melancholy

PLEAD	Make an earnest request
PROSPECT	Outlook for the future
PROTRUDED	Stuck out; extended beyond
RECESSED	Set back
RESPITE	A break
ROVING	Wandering about; going from place to place

SATCHEL	Small bag, sometimes with a shoulder strap
SCARCE	Insufficient to satisfy the need or demand
SCURRIED	Scampered or ran hastily
SENTRY	Guard; watch
SHINNY	Climb by using both hands and legs for gripping
SILOS	Airtight pits or towers in which fodder is stored

SKEPTICAL	Doubtful; not easily persuaded or convinced
SPINY	Covered with thorns or prickles
STOCKY	Having a sturdy form or build
SUBDUED	Quieted; less active than usual
TOILING	Working with exhausting labor or effort
TREMBLING	Shaking involuntarily with quick, short movements as from fear, excitement, or cold

TWINED	Interwoven; wrapped around
UNERRINGLY	Without mistakes
VACANT	Empty
VANTAGE	Position that provides a clear, broad view
VENTILATION	System that circulates air
VENTURED	Dared to do something dangerous or risky

VIGOROUS	Strong; active; robust
WEARILY	In a tired or worn-out manner
WRITHING	Making twisting or turning movements
YIELDED	Gave way

INEXORABLE	PERSPIRATION	IRRELEVANTLY	INLAID	SKEPTICAL
EPIDEMIC	EAVES	FRINGES	EMERGED	FUTILE
INCURRING	SATCHEL	FREE SPACE	HARROW	TOILING
DEFECTIVE	PEDDLER	INDIGNANTLY	HESITATED	FLUTTERED
FILTERING	MANIPULATED	ASTONISHED	AGITATED	ARTIFICIAL

Mrs Frisby Vocabulary

DELIBERATELY	ILLUSION	UNERRINGLY	EXPEDITION	INEXTRICABLY
DREADFULLY	GALE	CURSORY	STOCKY	CAPTIVITY
INCINERATOR	CONVERGED	FREE SPACE	WRITHING	DEBRIS
SHINNY	COLANDER	CONFER	CONCEALED	ASTUTE
CONSTERNATION	GRAVELY	SILOS	RESPITE	CONTOUR

Mrs Frisby Vocabulary

COMRADESHIP	ABREAST	DELIBERATELY	RECESSED	CIRCUMSTANCES
IRRELEVANTLY	WEARILY	VENTILATION	SUBDUED	INEXTRICABLY
DISPATCHED	VANTAGE	FREE SPACE	CONVERGED	PLEAD
EPIDEMIC	TOILING	AGITATED	CRYPTICALLY	TWINED
SKEPTICAL	EMERGED	RESPITE	SHINNY	VIGOROUS

Mrs Frisby Vocabulary

YIELDED	WRITHING	SATCHEL	FRINGES	FUTILE
ASTONISHED	TREMBLING	DICTATED	INCINERATOR	HERMIT
COLANDER	GRAVELY	FREE SPACE	COMPILED	ARTIFICIAL
HYPODERMIC	PLAINTIVE	CORRIDOR	BEWILDERMENT	MANIPULATED
FILTERING	UNERRINGLY	DESPAIRINGLY	DEFECTIVE	INEXORABLE

CYNICAL	HYPODERMIC	DISCONTENT	CONCEALED	SILOS
FLUTTERED	SKEPTICAL	PROTRUDED	ADMONISHED	SATCHEL
SUBDUED	CORDIAL	FREE SPACE	ILLUSION	DRONING
COMPILED	CONSTERNATION	PLEAD	EAVES	SPINY
DEFECTIVE	INEXORABLE	CORRIDOR	INLAID	ASTUTE

Mrs Frisby Vocabulary

EXERT	GRAVELY	VIGOROUS	EAVESDROP	AGITATED
INCINERATOR	ADJOURNED	TWINED	PLAINTIVE	WEARILY
ASTONISHED	AUTHORITATIVELY	FREE SPACE	HESITATED	DESCENT
TOILING	EXPEDITION	EPIDEMIC	CLUTTERED	CONVERGED
MANIPULATED	INEXTRICABLY	PEDDLER	DISPATCHED	WRITHING

CONCEALED	SCURRIED	CLUTTERED	VENTILATION	ABRUPTLY
ROVING	IMPASSE	YIELDED	GRAVELY	TREMBLING
CYNICAL	IRRELEVANTLY	FREE SPACE	STOCKY	BEWILDERMENT
VENTURED	FILTERING	SHINNY	AUTHORITATIVELY	CONVERGED
DICTATED	WRITHING	EXERT	INEXTRICABLY	PEDDLER

Mrs Frisby Vocabulary

DESPAIRINGLY	HERMIT	CORDIAL	INCLINE	INCURRING
CAPTIVITY	PARTITIONS	SATCHEL	PROTRUDED	PROSPECT
VACANT	SENTRY	FREE SPACE	ABREAST	AGITATED
ASTONISHED	FRINGES	FLUTTERED	PLAINTIVE	DESCENT
PLEAD	DISPATCHED	CRYPTICALLY	HYPODERMIC	PESSIMIST

Mrs Frisby Vocabulary

DESPAIRINGLY	VANTAGE	CONCEALED	DESCENT	PEDDLER
CAPTIVITY	CORRIDOR	ABRUPTLY	IRRELEVANTLY	CULTIVATED
UNERRINGLY	CURSORY	FREE SPACE	AGITATED	SKEPTICAL
WEARILY	INEXTRICABLY	BEWILDERMENT	DREADFULLY	SPINY
DELIBERATELY	GALE	HERMIT	CONVERGED	EAVESDROP

Mrs Frisby Vocabulary

WRITHING	DUSK	FILTERING	DICTATED	EXPEDITION
SCURRIED	CONFER	PESSIMIST	DRONING	TOILING
ARTIFICIAL	TWINED	FREE SPACE	MANIPULATED	INLAID
DISPATCHED	YIELDED	CYNICAL	FUTILE	PLEAD
PROSPECT	RECESSED	RESPITE	HARROW	PARTITIONS

PESSIMIST	EMERGED	SUBDUED	COMPILED	MANIPULATED
TOILING	INCURRING	CULTIVATED	RECESSED	COLANDER
ROVING	FILTERING	FREE SPACE	TWINED	EXERT
CORRIDOR	CONFER	SENTRY	CONVERGED	INDIGNANTLY
DISCONTENT	SKEPTICAL	HESITATED	DRONING	HARROW

UNERRINGLY	HYPODERMIC	FLUTTERED	ABREAST	SATCHEL
GRAVELY	GALE	ADMONISHED	WEARILY	FRINGES
DUSK	INKLING	FREE SPACE	INEXTRICABLY	IMPASSE
VANTAGE	INCINERATOR	CRYPTICALLY	CURSORY	DREADFULLY
SPINY	INEXORABLE	ARTIFICIAL	PEDDLER	DESCENT

DESPAIRINGLY	TWINED	PROTRUDED	DEBRIS	PLAINTIVE
INLAID	DISPATCHED	INDIGNANTLY	COLANDER	SUBDUED
INCINERATOR	TOILING	FREE SPACE	AUTHORITATIVELY	VENTILATION
SHINNY	EXPEDITION	HYPODERMIC	CIRCUMSTANCES	ADJOURNED
CLUTTERED	DESCENT	PEDDLER	HESITATED	GALE

Mrs Frisby Vocabulary

EAVES	DICTATED	IMPASSE	COMPILED	WRITHING
BEWILDERMENT	SKEPTICAL	ADMONISHED	EXERT	WEARILY
COMRADESHIP	INCLINE	FREE SPACE	SPINY	ABREAST
CULTIVATED	TREMBLING	DREADFULLY	CONCEALED	INCURRING
CONTOUR	DEFECTIVE	PLEAD	INEXTRICABLY	RECESSED

Mrs Frisby Vocabulary

AGITATED	PLEAD	DRONING	ABREAST	PERSPIRATION
FLUTTERED	EMERGED	RECESSED	ARTIFICIAL	UNERRINGLY
EAVES	INCLINE	FREE SPACE	TWINED	DUSK
MANIPULATED	CONTOUR	ASTUTE	CAPTIVITY	INCINERATOR
DISPATCHED	VENTILATION	SCURRIED	ROVING	CULTIVATED

Mrs Frisby Vocabulary

PROSPECT	CONVERGED	PLAINTIVE	FILTERING	AUTHORITATIVELY
ILLUSION	SHINNY	COMPILED	DELIBERATELY	DICTATED
IRRELEVANTLY	EPIDEMIC	FREE SPACE	VACANT	DEBRIS
INLAID	GRAVELY	SUBDUED	VANTAGE	CONCEALED
IMPASSE	EAVESDROP	HERMIT	YIELDED	VIGOROUS

Mrs Frisby Vocabulary

CLUTTERED	HYPODERMIC	IMPASSE	EXPEDITION	YIELDED
ROVING	CONFER	DUSK	CONVERGED	UNERRINGLY
CYNICAL	CURSORY	FREE SPACE	DESPAIRINGLY	COMPILED
PLEAD	GALE	INDIGNANTLY	INEXTRICABLY	HERMIT
DICTATED	DELIBERATELY	INCURRING	FRINGES	TOILING

Mrs Frisby Vocabulary

HARROW	SKEPTICAL	FILTERING	EPIDEMIC	SCARCE
GRAVELY	TWINED	PESSIMIST	SPINY	ILLUSION
CONSTERNATION	COLANDER	FREE SPACE	INCLINE	PLAINTIVE
AUTHORITATIVELY	RESPITE	CULTIVATED	ELEGANTLY	ADJOURNED
ABRUPTLY	SILOS	PARTITIONS	VANTAGE	DISPATCHED

Mrs Frisby Vocabulary

VACANT	PLEAD	INEXTRICABLY	AGITATED	ADMONISHED
IMPASSE	TREMBLING	BEWILDERMENT	TOILING	EXERT
DREADFULLY	CONFER	FREE SPACE	ADJOURNED	VIGOROUS
AUTHORITATIVELY	RECESSED	DRONING	PROTRUDED	CULTIVATED
GRAVELY	CONTOUR	CORDIAL	PARTITIONS	INDIGNANTLY

Mrs Frisby Vocabulary

EMERGED	SUBDUED	SCARCE	DESCENT	VANTAGE
CAPTIVITY	HESITATED	DEBRIS	DISCONTENT	IRRELEVANTLY
HARROW	UNERRINGLY	FREE SPACE	CLUTTERED	YIELDED
RESPITE	PERSPIRATION	CONSTERNATION	COLANDER	VENTILATION
EXPEDITION	EPIDEMIC	PEDDLER	EAVES	CRYPTICALLY

Mrs Frisby Vocabulary

SPINY	PLEAD	WRITHING	YIELDED	TREMBLING
TWINED	DESPAIRINGLY	ILLUSION	HESITATED	SCURRIED
STOCKY	ASTONISHED	FREE SPACE	INCLINE	FLUTTERED
VENTILATION	SATCHEL	ARTIFICIAL	FUTILE	DREADFULLY
TOILING	SENTRY	EAVESDROP	AGITATED	CIRCUMSTANCES

Mrs Frisby Vocabulary

PARTITIONS	CRYPTICALLY	EMERGED	HERMIT	ADMONISHED
ROVING	ADJOURNED	DELIBERATELY	RECESSED	CONTOUR
SKEPTICAL	CORRIDOR	FREE SPACE	CULTIVATED	PESSIMIST
HARROW	INLAID	CYNICAL	WEARILY	DUSK
BEWILDERMENT	COLANDER	DISPATCHED	DICTATED	DISCONTENT

DREADFULLY	ADJOURNED	SATCHEL	CYNICAL	INCURRING
FUTILE	CONFER	EPIDEMIC	DUSK	PLEAD
ABREAST	SPINY	FREE SPACE	DEBRIS	TREMBLING
DRONING	IMPASSE	ROVING	FILTERING	DESPAIRINGLY
INCINERATOR	SILOS	CLUTTERED	SKEPTICAL	WEARILY

Mrs Frisby Vocabulary

GRAVELY	VIGOROUS	CONVERGED	YIELDED	EMERGED
PLAINTIVE	EXERT	VACANT	GALE	BEWILDERMENT
FRINGES	SCARCE	FREE SPACE	INCLINE	TOILING
COLANDER	CONSTERNATION	COMRADESHIP	PROTRUDED	ABRUPTLY
INLAID	VENTURED	DISCONTENT	EAVES	HARROW

CONCEALED	INLAID	EXPEDITION	DEFECTIVE	TREMBLING
PARTITIONS	CURSORY	DEBRIS	DUSK	CORDIAL
CAPTIVITY	RECESSED	FREE SPACE	FLUTTERED	DELIBERATELY
COLANDER	GALE	ABRUPTLY	EPIDEMIC	WRITHING
TWINED	EXERT	INEXORABLE	HARROW	SILOS

HESITATED	DREADFULLY	AUTHORITATIVELY	ROVING	HYPODERMIC
RESPITE	ABREAST	ILLUSION	DESCENT	SCURRIED
PESSIMIST	FUTILE	FREE SPACE	COMPILED	INEXTRICABLY
GRAVELY	DISPATCHED	SCARCE	CLUTTERED	EMERGED
CONSTERNATION	MANIPULATED	PLAINTIVE	ADJOURNED	HERMIT

Mrs Frisby Vocabulary

PROSPECT	SHINNY	ADMONISHED	TREMBLING	DISCONTENT
UNERRINGLY	CULTIVATED	COLANDER	RECESSED	PLAINTIVE
FILTERING	HERMIT	FREE SPACE	INKLING	INEXTRICABLY
VENTILATION	PERSPIRATION	PLEAD	DESPAIRINGLY	SPINY
CONCEALED	INEXORABLE	HARROW	ABRUPTLY	AGITATED

Mrs Frisby Vocabulary

YIELDED	DESCENT	CRYPTICALLY	HESITATED	DEFECTIVE
CORDIAL	HYPODERMIC	GRAVELY	INCINERATOR	CONTOUR
WEARILY	MANIPULATED	FREE SPACE	CONVERGED	ROVING
DISPATCHED	INLAID	INCLINE	PESSIMIST	SKEPTICAL
FLUTTERED	DEBRIS	VANTAGE	VENTURED	SATCHEL

Mrs Frisby Vocabulary

SATCHEL	INKLING	INDIGNANTLY	SCARCE	ELEGANTLY
INCINERATOR	UNERRINGLY	CORDIAL	CULTIVATED	ARTIFICIAL
VENTILATION	CONFER	FREE SPACE	RECESSED	INCURRING
DEFECTIVE	EPIDEMIC	MANIPULATED	INCLINE	ASTUTE
CAPTIVITY	SUBDUED	WRITHING	INEXORABLE	VIGOROUS

Mrs Frisby Vocabulary

HYPODERMIC	FUTILE	EMERGED	VACANT	EXERT
VENTURED	HERMIT	INLAID	RESPITE	DREADFULLY
AUTHORITATIVELY	SHINNY	FREE SPACE	CONVERGED	DICTATED
DISCONTENT	HESITATED	EXPEDITION	SPINY	ABREAST
INEXTRICABLY	EAVESDROP	IMPASSE	GALE	PEDDLER

Mrs Frisby Vocabulary

ADJOURNED	SILOS	EXERT	FILTERING	VANTAGE
SPINY	INCLINE	DESPAIRINGLY	SHINNY	PERSPIRATION
CIRCUMSTANCES	CULTIVATED	FREE SPACE	FRINGES	IRRELEVANTLY
EAVESDROP	HESITATED	DEBRIS	DISCONTENT	CONCEALED
CONTOUR	CONSTERNATION	STOCKY	CURSORY	ASTONISHED

Mrs Frisby Vocabulary

EMERGED	PLEAD	ADMONISHED	CRYPTICALLY	PARTITIONS
DUSK	ROVING	CORRIDOR	INDIGNANTLY	UNERRINGLY
RESPITE	PEDDLER	FREE SPACE	CAPTIVITY	DEFECTIVE
BEWILDERMENT	WRITHING	AUTHORITATIVELY	HERMIT	EXPEDITION
COMRADESHIP	SUBDUED	DISPATCHED	CORDIAL	INKLING